Tuned
and Under Tension

Tuned
and Under Tension

The Recent Poetry
of W. D. Snodgrass

Edited by Philip Raisor

DELAWARE

Newark: University of Delaware Press
London: Associated University Presses

Associated University Presses
440 Forsgate Drive
Cranbury, NJ 08512

Associated University Presses
16 Barter Street
London WC1A 2AH, England

Associated University Presses
P.O. Box 338, Port Credit
Mississauga, Ontario
Canada L5G 4L8

The paper used in this publication meets the requirements
of the American National Standard for Permanence of Paper
for Printed Library Materials Z39.48-1984.

Library of Congress Cataloging-in-Publication Data

Tuned and under tension : the recent poetry of W.D. Snodgrass / edited by Philip Raisor.
    p.   cm.
Includes bibliographical references and index.
ISBN 0-87413-659-8 (alk. paper)
    1. Snodgrass, W. D. (William De Witt), 1926–   —Criticism and interpretation. I. Raisor, Philip, 1938– .
PS3537.N32Z89   1998
811'.54—dc21   98-18956
                                                                              CIP

PRINTED IN THE UNITED STATES OF AMERICA

for my parents, who began,
for Juanita, who continued,
keeping the strings

Keeping the strings
Tuned and under tension, we gradually
Pare away, while playing constantly,
All excess from behind the tempered face.

—W. D. Snodgrass, "Regraduating the Lute"

Contents

Foreword

Easily one of the greatest pleasures I have known in my time
at *The Southern Review* has been the opportunity to publish
W. D. Snodgrass, and he has generously nourished that pleasure
for the past ten years with poems, memoirs, and critical essays
. . . as well as the nonce genre to which "Disgracing Are Verse"
might be said to belong. When I arrived in Baton Rouge in 1983,
I had already been an admirer of Snodgrass's poetry for many
years—as far back as the appearance of *Heart's Needle* in 1959;
or maybe I should say my admiration dates from even earlier,
but if I said so, I would then have to go on to acknowledge that
in its first stages the admiration was more for the figure he cut
as a poet than for the actual poetry, which I doubt I had read
before the book publication. The refrain line in one of the *Heart's
Needle* poems—"These Trees Stand. . ."—declares that "Snodgrass is walking through the universe," and that is how I like to
think of him from my first acquaintance with his existence as a
poet. This was in 1951–55, when I was an undergraduate at the
University of Iowa and (for at least part of that time) he was in
the Writers' Workshop. What the locale of "These Trees
Stand . . ." was I cannot say, but I can confirm that one had the
sense that this person walking through the universe of Iowa City,
fortuitously named *Snodgrass*, was the genuine article—the
Poet. "Ah, did you once see Snodgrass plain . . ."—it was perhaps not quite a Browningesque sense of wonderment one felt
(and in memory still feels) seeing him striding along Clinton
Street and into Kenny's Bar just opposite the campus, but it was
not altogether different from that; and it was very exciting to
think that one of those mysterious and godlike people whose
writing appeared in the anthologies of literature classes was
among us in the flesh.

A quotation from Robert Lowell on the dustcover of my copy
of *Heart's Needle* says of Snodgrass, "He flowered in the most

sterile of sterile places, a post war, cold war midwestern university's workshop for graduate student poets," yet this is not what Snodgrass himself remembered of those days when he was finding himself as a poet. Shortly before sending a splendid memoir of his years in Iowa City—"A Liberal Education: Mentors, Fomenters and Tormentors"—to us at *The Southern Review*, Snodgrass wrote describing the work in progress: "The piece I'm trying to finish now has to do with college after the war—the Iowa Workshops, with a good bit of attention to Lowell, Jarrell and Berryman who were my teachers there. (My God, was I lucky!)" I recall all this about Snodgrass plain in the most sterile of sterile places—and his own sense of great good luck in having been there—to suggest what many of us must feel: that his luck was what he made it and that he flowered in the most sterile of places because it was his self-chosen destiny to do so. By his own testimony, Snodgrass didn't know he was a poet when he arrived in Iowa City, but when one looks back over the half century of dedication to poetry since the idea first dawned on him, the sense of his always having been a poet—or destined to be one—is very strong. "Even the wisest man grows tense. / With some sort of violence," Yeats writes in "Under Ben Bulben," "Before he can accomplish fate, / Know his work or choose his mate." We commonly think of fate as something that descends on us from without rather than something we accomplish from within, but Heraclitus says, "A man's character is his destiny" (his *daimon* in Greek), and I cannot escape the feeling that Snodgrass's long career has been a matter of his accomplishing fate, which is to say that his *daimon* has been, from the beginning, inescapably that of the poet.

I cite Yeats deliberately, for he, more than anyone else in our time, lived the life of the poet and gave expression to it both inside and outside the poetry. As "The First Principle" in his "General Information for My Work," Yeats declares, "A poet writes always of his personal life, in his finest work out of its tragedy, whatever it be, remorse, lost love, or mere loneliness," but, he continues, "he is never the bundle of accident and incoherence that sits down to breakfast; he has been reborn as an idea, something intended, complete." This notion of the poet as "an idea, something intended, complete" and of poetry of both craft and vocation—hard work and the highest of callings—may be old-fashioned, but it has animated Snodgrass's career for going on fifty years now.

Is it any wonder that we rejoice every time something new arrives in the offices of *The Southern Review* from W. D. Snodgrass?

JAMES OLNEY

Acknowledgments

I WISH TO THANK MY COLLEAGUES WHO CONTRIBUTED TO THIS COLLECTION of essays. Their enthusiasm for the project was constant encouragement to achieve for the whole book the quality evident in their individual contributions. I would also like to thank Old Dominion University for providing me a semester leave. I am grateful to the University of Delaware for its support of the cover design. I am also grateful to Bruce Weigl and Philip Hoy for their helpful suggestions on the manuscript. Kathy and W. D. Snodgrass have been persistently kind, and Bernard Benstock's kindly counsel and professionalism over the years was, as it should be, by both word and example.

Finally, I wish to express my thanks to the following for their permission to reproduce copyright material:

DeLoss McGraw for the images "W. D. Shields Himself" and "W. D.'s Midnight Carnival Friends," and Robert Perrine, publisher, for the poems in W. D.'s Midnight Carnival, Artra Publishing, 1988;

Arnold Stein for an extended excerpt from "On Elizabethan Wit," reprinted by permission of Studies in English Literature 1500–1900 1, 1 (Winter 1961);

Paul Gaston for an extended excerpt from "W. D. Snodgrass and The Fuehrer Bunker: An Interview," Papers on Language and Literature 13, 3 (Summer 1997). Copyright (c) 1977 by the Board of Trustees, Southern Illinois University. Reprinted by permission of the publisher;

W. D. Snodgrass: Excerpts from various poems copyright (c) 1993 by W. D. Snodgrass. Reprinted from Each in His Season with the permission of BOA Editions, Ltd.;

W. D. Snodgrass: excerpts from various poems copyright (c) 1995 by W. D. Snodgrass. Reprinted from The Fuehrer Bunker: The Completed Cycle, with permission of BOA Editions, Ltd.;

W. D. Snodgrass for poems in The Death of Cock Robin, University of Delaware Press, 1989, with permission of the author.

Tuned
and Under Tension

Introduction

I ONCE ASKED W. D. SNODGRASS HOW VALUABLE HE THOUGHT THE eccentric was. I had been thinking about his collection of essays in *In Radical Pursuit* and several eccentric characters in his work: the boy made of meat, the nonspecialist professor in "April Inventory," Cock Robin and others. He said, "Depends on how *you* define the eccentric." I said, "As deviant from the customary." He smiled and said,

> Oh, in that case, it's liable to be very good indeed because the customary always involves limitations of vision, and unless you're saying something that people aren't generally saying there is almost no sense in saying it. Any society survives by limiting everybody's vision; it may also ruin itself by doing that. In any case, if you say something different, people aren't gonna like that and they're gonna see it as eccentric, where, in fact, it may be absolutely central.[1]

In his essays and interviews, Snodgrass has often been quite explicit about the "absolutely central" in his vision. He has noted at times that the disguises we choose most clearly reveal the darker sides of our personalities; at other times he has emphasized that sharing humanity's degradations is a prerequisite for understanding humanity's nobility; at others he has noted that a liberating nonsense often exposes more of a truth than does rational sense. More important than particular observations, however, is his constant attempt to understand the limit of conventional knowing and go beyond it.

I suppose we could say that Snodgrass's predilection for the eccentric is a customary poetic stance and one, in fact, characteristic of post-World War II poets. Charles Molesworth, in his fine survey of contemporary American poetry, identifies a bevy of poets—Bly, Kinnell, Ammons, O'Hara, Ginsberg, and Creeley— all born in 1926 or 1927, for whom "the language of poetry had to be 'against the grain,' not in any tepid sense of the 'loyal

opposition,' but in the most radical way they could manage."[2]
Maybe it's a generational thing, but Snodgrass, also born in 1926,
was as aware as the others of a need to jettison an "official" or
purported American hegemony and the accepted maxims of the
reigning academic poetry. His *Heart's Needle* (1959) was, as one
reviewer said, iconoclastic: Snodgrass "has simply junked
Pound's, Eliot's, and the imagists' dicta about the impersonality
of the poet. His subject is frankly himself."[3] With that, and along
with others in the late 50s and early 60s, Snodgrass brought
eccentricity into the mainstream.

But there is a difference between Snodgrass and many of his
contemporaries. Even in his poetry, much to the chagrin of his
critics, Snodgrass has refused to write the Pulitzer Prize-winning
Heart's Needle over and over. He has constantly sought different
subjects, forms, and angles of vision. In this sense, he has been
as eccentric with his own work as he has been with conventional
wisdom. The fact that he has gone from *Heart's Needle* and *After
Experience* to *The Fuehrer Bunker*, then to the collaboration
with the painter DeLoss McGraw in *W. D.'s Midnight Carnival*
and *The Death of Cock Robin*, all the while extending the *Bunker*
to its conclusion, goes against a predictable grain, and seems to
some commentators an unacceptable eccentricity.

The result has been that a number of critics have dismissed
the later poetry. An admirer of the early work, J. D. McClatchy,
for example, finds the latest poems "not only a disappointment
but a puzzle." And he asks: "Why would a poet with such gifts,
even in his search for diversity and new 'voices,' deliberately
parody those gifts and wreck a career?"[4] Thus, Snodgrass's post-
confessional collaborations with the painter McGraw and the
dramatic monologues of the *Bunker* are seen as anomalies and
misdirections.

But another part of the problem is the critical rancor that the
Bunker poems have evoked for the last twenty years. From their
appearance in the late 1970s to the present, Snodgrass's monologues have lead to accusations that he made the Nazis human
or sympathized with their emotional traumas. One early reviewer
commented that Snodgrass, whether he intended to or not, "has
made these godawful people (as in the case of Eva Braun) oddly
appealing. . . . I am not ready for that."[5] And another, more re-

cently, though he finds that Snodgrass in no way compromises with the Nazis, advises that, "with his task finished, he ought to get out of the bunker as fast as he can."[6] Such observations do not necessarily result from blatantly unsympathetic readings; they do, however, perpetuate the view that Snodgrass should get back to the persona of *Heart's Needle*.

Thus the reason for this collection (at least my motive for initiating it) is the historical fact that most of the critical work on Snodgrass concentrates on his early period. Very little has been done on the work he has been doing for the past twenty years. In other words, his reputation rests on his place in the confessional movement, and what appeared to be his rebellion against the moderns. Maybe McClatchy is correct we could say; maybe Snodgrass has wrecked his career. But that view should not stand without looking closely at the sustained body of work that Snodgrass has been doing (and continues to do) in the midst of dramatic changes in poetic taste and critical scrutiny.

I would say then that the material in this collection, all previously unpublished, is an entirely fresh look at W. D. Snodgrass. It constitutes close readings of the later poetry, principally *W. D.'s Midnight Carnival*, *The Death of Cock Robin*, *Each in His Season*, and the new *The Fuehrer Bunker* (eighty poems and re-visioned). Brenda Tremblay's interview with Snodgrass was the first one conducted after the publication of the new *Bunker*.

I did not ask the writers of these essays to reorient contemporary criticism. It would be an injustice to them to leave the impression that they set out in this direction or even that I gave them a map at all. I simply asked intelligent readers, and in several cases, practitioners, of poetry to respond as they chose to Snodgrass's later works. Therefore, the essays are more than my discoveries in them would suggest. Each is its own lively and often witty response to the taut, musical, and carefully formed structures of W. D. Snodgrass.

Yet these essays collectively confirm that Snodgrass did not lose his way in some Valley of Despond, but in rebelling against the prescribed limits of modernism (as set in the 1950s) actually sought to extend them. In an era which has consistently claimed the end of modernism, I think it is important to recognize not only that news of its death is premature but also that modernism has not yet been fully defined. For some writers it is still an active catalyst. Peter Makuck recognizes this in the first essay: "Although he helped change the direction away from modernist poetry, W. D. Snodgrass, in many ways, is still a modernist at heart. Like those exemplary writers James Joyce and Virginia Woolf, who also exploited conventions and forms, called into question literary traditions, and insisted on making readers reexamine received values and forms, Snodgrass takes nothing for granted, regards the past in his own way, and uses it to his own purposes."

The fact that Snodgrass is so deeply entrenched in the modernist tradition of creating his own universe makes it possible for him to constantly deconstruct and reconstruct the surface while preserving the underlying principle of organization. My point in the second essay of the collection is that this is, and always has been, Snodgrass's macrocosmic view. Zack Bowen and Fred Chappell, in their commentaries on the musical influences on Snodgrass's work, find it in the microcosm as well. For Bowen, the result in *The Fuehrer Bunker* is that the disparate voices of the Nazis are "like the conflicting melodic lines in Wagnerian opera or twentieth century classical music." But together they "form a chorus at once discordant, various, banal and lyrical, a single multiperspective on the inner tumult of off-base people. . . ." Chappell finds that the large section "Each in His Season" from the volume of that name "resembles a great many other modernist works: its surface looks ragtag and arbitrary, but the apprehension of an organizing principle reveals firm structural design. A string quartet of Schoenberg offers the same perplexities and resolution, as do Cubist paintings by Braque and Picasso."

What is the significance, one might ask, of recognizing that Snodgrass is both an antimodernist and a modernist, that he preserves the tension between the two, that, specifically, as Bernard Benstock states in his essay, Snodgrass "abandoned the modern poet's insistence on developing a single dominant voice," but preserved another "modernist credo . . . that each piece of art determines its own shape, form, style. . ."? One result, I think, is that it helps us understand Snodgrass's sense of experi-

mentation (he is, of course, one of the most experimental of contemporary poets). Snodgrass understands Pound's advice to
"make it new." Yet, he is fully aware of and engaged in the use
of Eliot's "tradition." We must see his individual tactics as part
of a broader strategy. His search for diversity, new voices, and his
use of irony must be seen in conjunction with his use of paradox,
wit, invention, musical and literary motifs, etc. But more than
that, such an approach makes it possible for Devon Miller-
Duggan and David Metzger to recognize that the meanings in
The Fuehrer Bunker are the result of specific kinds of interrelationships between craft and content and that inadequate readings result from the failure to appreciate those interrelationships.

Perhaps we can understand that Snodgrass's modernism,
which may be uniquely his, is firmly grounded in long thought
about that tradition and his relationship to it. His view is certainly not the limited version that Jonathan Holden claims is
being effectively dismantled by contemporary poets—the view
that confines modernism to an impersonal voice, an elitist intel-
lectualism, and an art for art's sake subject matter.[7] That Model
T, rooted in the symbolist practices of Baudelaire and Verlaine,
has, says Holden, run out of fuel, and Snodgrass would agree.
As he said, over twenty years ago, in *In Radical Pursuit*, "Daring
as this intellectual and artistic revolution was, it reached artists
of my generation in a seriously debased form. It always had a
number of regressive and backward tendencies which, as the
movement passed to second-rate minds and became institutionalized, became dominant and oppressive."

Forward-looking, Snodgrass would find closer alignment with
Robert Pinsky's modernism—its innovative spirit and commit-
ment to the particulars of a physical world which a precise language could capture.[8] From his discursive analysis of Eliot,
Williams, Crane, Pound, Stevens, Yeats, and others, Pinsky sees
that certain conventions continue into the contemporary period.
These conventions—fresh applications of the dramatic monologue, evocative rather than descriptive language, innovations
with form, and a "cool" surrealism—are not at all alien to Snodgrass's practices in his later work in particular.

But a view which more closely approximates Snodgrass's modernism is that delineated by Albert Gelpi in his recent essay "The

Genealogy of Postmodernism: Contemporary American Poetry."[9] Gelpi finds that modernism is not only High Modernism of 1910–1925 which emphasized the autonomy of art, but also includes the later works of Eliot, Pound, H. D., Stevens, and Williams, which recover the connection between art and life. Both are justifiably linked, says Gelpi, because the key to modernism is the affirmation of the imagination, and that can be done in both an autonomous art and a mimetic one. Gelpi argues that postmodern thinking terminates the link, and wherever we see the imagination acting as an "agency of coherence" we know we are still at the center of modernist thinking (a thinking deeply rooted in both the romantic ecstasy and irony of the nineteenth century). Says Gelpi, the working of the modernist imagination makes it possible for poets to express "a passionate desire to press limits and extend possibilities, an insistence that language penetrate rather than maintain surfaces, a compulsion to fathom the mystery linking subject and object, person and person, word and thing in a constructive act of signification." Unlike postmodernism, says Gelpi, this version of modernism (which he labels "Neoromantic" in the contemporary period) retains its "rage for order" and its premise that a work of art can influence psychological, moral, political, and religious consciousness.

Snodgrass has indeed given thought to this. Once asked if the world and art were postmodern, were, in fact, unfinished, having neither intrinsic order nor meaning, Snodgrass replied:

> That any statement about whether the world has intrinsic meaning or not seems to me meaningless, because we can't imagine the world unimagined. We only know the world as different people have experienced it. To say that a world not experienced by somebody has or does not have meaning is simply a meaningless statement. In a work of art, I am concerned about whether the thing comes to have meaning as a whole because it seems to me that every piece I admire very much does have that.[10]

In fact, Snodgrass's The Death of Cock Robin—on one level, all about the supposed death and possible resurrection of the poetic imagination—demonstrates that the imagination is not only validated by its encounter with experience, but also by its capacity to give form to that experience. In a concluding poem in which

W. D. is disguised as Cock Robin and both poet and imagination
are one, W. D. says,

> I ride the pulse that swells
> Lips, nails, all feverish parts;
> I wear the blushing scarlet
> Alphabet that spells
> The blazing braille of hearts,
> The shorted shorts of the harlot,
> Virgin, housewife, starlet.
>
> I doppelgang some grander
> Land that schizophrenics
> Colonize from earth,
> One with the salamander,
> With that flaming phoenix
> Or lodgepole pine whose clenched cones need
> The forest fire to cast their seed.

Deep in the interior of body and mind, of language and invention,
the imagination remains inextricably linked with the myths of
eternal return. It is essentially the form-getting and form-giving
power.

Yet, truly imaginative, Snodgrass includes the postmodern.
Discordance, discontinuity, and rupture are held together, not by
a system of ideas which explains away the differences, but by an
ardent desire to affirm their indissolubility. The only way for
Snodgrass to do that is to include in his world the suffering
child, divorced father, the abandoned lovers, the paintings, legends, myths, fairy tales which are artifacts of pain, the exuber-
ance of owls, the energy of dance, the ancient villains, and the
modern Nazis, everything human, including the postmodern
sensibility. Snodgrass is as aware as L-A-N-G-U-A-G-E poets of
the fissures between word and object; he has as much doubt
about ontological reality as Charles Bernstein. Beckett's narrator
in WATT claims that our constructions of all systems are no more
than pacifiers for unsatisfied cravings. So too does Snodgrass.
His Hitler "fed sick on sugartits" and admiring Stalin's appetite
for destruction ("nothing sticks in that man's craw") constructs
a thousand-year reich. But it does not dissolve the discords. The
absurd, alienated, random remain important ingredients in the

Snodgrass mix. In a "House of Horrors" where confusion reigns, we live in

> our elevated pit and black hole
> where all light and energies rush in
> and fail; yet, yes, but once inside
> and it gets hard to tell it from
> Versailles' vast Hall of Mirrors
> where cataclysmic peace broke out;
> as if the polished granite pillars of
> burnt Persepolis gave back your face,
> the walls of Altamira your nickname
> and secret vices; as if the air
> held all sound waves created
> since the first big bang, a sort of
> tape recorder under your best bed or
> Quaker meeting in the craphouse—
> welcome, in the end then, to the great
> kakangelist's big top and revival
> for the psalm and badspel of our days:
> the world is much the way the world
> wants; it's too late for you to change.
> It is as if it's just like what it is.

We live in a metaphor on top of a simile inside of our being, and must choose how to live. Instead of Beckett's path, however, Snodgrass chooses Whitman's.

In his most recent essay ("Whitman's Self-song,") Snodgrass set out to investigate "not only the relation between Whitman's life and beliefs but, more significant, the resulting eccentric structure and style of his works."[11] The eccentricity of Whitman's works for Snodgrass is apparent everywhere, in "his characteristic poetic structures, his blend of conventions, genres, and points of view, his subject matter and vocabulary, eccentric syntax, distinctive prosodic and rhythmic practices." This eccentricity is characterized by its openness, its "democracy," in which all things that the mind encounters are absorbed and included. Nothing is marginalized. Whitman, says Snodgrass, defined the self only by its scope; "he insisted that he *was* whatever he encountered. This sense of affirmation changed not only his *Weltanschauung*, but also the structure and style of his works."

Snodgrass's analysis of Whitman is self-reflexive. What Snodgrass finds in his mentor, we find in him. The affirmation, inclusiveness, diversity, expansiveness, and the restless drive for both form and new forms are all parts of Snodgrass's poetics. Such recognition has led Anne Colwell in the last essay in this collection to a reading of *The Fuehrer Bunker* that opens further for us Snodgrass's own eccentricity and its purpose and richness in his work.

Perhaps, such steady and reiterative focus on the later works of W. D. Snodgrass makes this collection an "introduction"—and I hope it will be conceived of in this way. Each writer has taken a work or theme (music, wit, evil, etc.) which has led him/her into the complexities of Snodgrass's dense layerings of content and technique to open new areas of understanding. At the same time, these essays suggest possibilities for further studies in Snodgrass's use of music, the stage, translated material, history, form, and metrics. But this volume also provides a corrective to the view that Snodgrass can be divided into parts—the first half and the second. His vision is seamless. It is designed to expand and expand. In Snodgrass's universe all selves and all isms are there, under tension perhaps, but finely tuned by the artist's craft.

Notes

1. Philip Raisor, "Framing Portraits: An Interview with W. D. Snodgrass," *The Southern Review* 26 (Winter 1990): 71.

2. Charles Molesworth, *The Fierce Embrace: A Study of Contemporary American Poetry* (Columbia and London: University of Missouri Press, 1979), 79.

3. Daniel G. Hoffman, "Arrivals and Rebirths," *The Sewanee Review* 68, 1 (Winter 1960): 172.

4. J. D. McClatchy, "W. D. Snodgrass: The Mild Reflective Art," *The Poetry of W. D. Snodgrass: Everything Human*, ed. Stephen Haven (Ann Arbor: University of Michigan Press, 1993), 143.

5. John N. Morris, "Eight Books from Small Presses," *Ohio Review* 19, 1 (Winter 1978): 106.

6. Larry Levis, "Waiting for the End of the World: Snodgrass and *The Fuehrer Bunker*," *The Poetry of W. D. Snodgrass: Everything Human*, ed. Stephen Haven (Ann Arbor: University of Michigan Press, 1993), 281.

7. Jonathan Holden, *The Fate of American Poetry* (Athens and London: University of Georgia Press, 1991), 59.

8. Robert Pinsky, *The Situation of Poetry: Contemporary Poetry and Its Tradition* (Princeton: Princeton University Press, 1976), 3–6.

9. *The Southern Review* 26, 3 (Summer 1990): 517–41.

10. Raisor, 79.

11. *The Southern Review* 32, 3 (Summer 1996): 572–602.

Dangerous Difference: W. D. Snodgrass's
The Death Of Cock Robin

PETER MAKUCK

JUST WHAT HATH SNODGRASS WROUGHT? AN ATTEMPT TO ATTACH A
label could easily have me sounding like old Polonius pontifi-
cating before the Players ("tragical-historical, tragical-comical-
historical-pastoral"), hedging bets by mixing this with that. But
it's safe to say that Snodgrass has fulfilled the Poundian impera-
tive and made it—whatever it is—new, astoundingly new, this
narrative sequence of formally challenging poems that feature
Cock Robin as a fugitive songster who is furtively helped by
his friend, W. D., sheltered by the Storm Family, but pursued
relentlessly by Mr. Evil, a government operative, and finally ter-
minated with extreme prejudice in a police state where indifferent, or cowardly, or hostile neighbors look on.

If what I gather from overheard academic conversations is true,
i.e., that postmodernism blankly looks upon the world with a
certain smug knowingness that curdles feeling, choice, and responsibility into glib irony, and is obsessed with surfaces (as if
meaning and depth were a pitiful form of *nostalgie de Dieu*),
then *The Death of Cock Robin* might represent one of the last
heartbeats of modernism, for it has many of the hallmarks of
that aesthetic and worldview: intricate design, serious moral and
aesthetic concerns, a sympathy for the abyss, themes of exile and
loneliness, tension between high culture and pop culture, the
idea of art as a sanctuary from devaluation, redefined terms of
heroism (from heroism of deed to heroism of consciousness), a
separate peace, or the notion that the world is beyond changing.

The modernists often used existing stories, mythologies, and
poetic forms for their own ends; that applies here. Even though
the book opens with a traditional *requiescat in pace*, with the

26

narrative persona W. D. placing "this small vase, / of blossom" to honor "the place / you rest," *The Death of Cock Robin* is not really an elegy or a nursery rhyme; yet it is nonetheless elegiac, that is to say dangerously disruptive in the way of Mark Antony when he mourned the death of Caesar while indicting power lust in those who assassinated him. Traditional elegies have also been disruptive. Two of the four great English lamentations go on the attack: Milton, in "Lycidas," uses Edward King's death to target a morally tainted clergy as well as protest worldliness ("Fame is no plant that grows on mortal soil"); Shelley, in "Adonais," excoriates heartless reviewers for the death of Keats. In our own century T. S. Eliot dedicates "The Love Song of J. Alfred Prufrock" to his friend Jean Verdenal killed in the Great War, leading us to consider this poem, as well as *The Waste Land* which begins with "The Burial of the Dead," as a veiled elegy on modern life as Dantean hell, a death in life where London shades merely exist, smogged in by boredom, prisoners of their "Unreal City." Ezra Pound and Wilfred Owen also utilized the elegy as a way of mourning civilization itself, a civilization either dying or already dead. Faulkner's *The Bear* and Fitzgerald's *The Great Gatsby* are modernist classic novels that, among other things, can be regarded as elegies lamenting the death of American innocence while indicting the causes of that death.

Although he helped change the direction away from modernist poetry, W. D. Snodgrass, in many ways, is still a modernist at heart. Like those exemplary writers James Joyce and Virginia Woolf, who also exploited conventions and forms and called into question literary traditions, and insisted on making readers reexamine received values and forms, Snodgrass takes nothing for granted, regards the past in his own way, and uses it to his own purposes. Consider, for a moment, the revisionist possibilities in his model, the "Mother Goose" original, seemingly innocent of implication, in which Cock Robin is accidentally shot at the dinner that celebrates his marriage to Jenny Wren. Sparrow is the immediate cause of Cock Robin's death, Cuckoo the remote, for it was Cuckoo whom Sparrow was actually aiming at with his bow and arrow. Point of view being problematic even in nursery rhymes, it is difficult to say how the arrow strayed; indeed, the Mother Goose narrator waffles, giving us multiple choices and pre-echoing a modernist preoccupation:

His aim then he took
    But he took it not right;
His skill was not good,
    Or he shot in a fright.

For reasons unknown, the narrator never lingers on the character
of the Cuckoo, whose behavior is certainly suspicious; all we get
are the cold facts, no probing whys. The cuckoo simply crashed
the celebration, "made a great rout," grabbed hold of Jenny, and
"pulled her about." But why? Just drunk and having fun? Possibly. Unmotivated malice? Angry because he had been denied
tenure and promotion? An intriguing angle, but simple, too simple. A major problem is the absence of an autopsy. Sparrow, you
see, might not have been the only shooter. In fact, Cock Robin
was probably taken out by a mini-crossbow, a tiny bolt that
would hide itself in his feathers. And the teller might want to
make Sparrow's fatal shot *appear* an accident. We're talking alle-
giances, group identity. People forget, for example, that the president of the college where Cock Robin was a salaried songster
was an élitist penguin. Isn't it possible that Cuckoo was paid
to create a diversion? Think about the contemporary political
climate. Isn't it likely that some narrow-minded birds of a feather
would be enraged to see a robin from a respectable old English
family marry some dark, yappy little wren from the Carolinas?
Old attitudes change slowly. You see how this could go? Or am I
reading too much into a simple tale of—what? The best
laid schemes o' robins and wrens gang aft a-gley? *Cherchez le
coucou?*

To a certain sensibility, the famous question of who killed Cock
Robin invites wonderful possibilities, but the subtle kind of cultural conspiracy Snodgrass has in mind would put someone like
Oliver Stone out of his league. Given his abiding thematic con-
cerns, especially the bloody struggle of the fittest to survive, the
terror of state surveillance, and total police control sounded in
The Fuehrer Bunker, W. D. Snodgrass's seriocomic choice of the
Mother Goose nursery rhyme is a masterstroke. For one thing,
we have a violent, a seemingly accidental death. But now imagine
a killer who isn't as forthcoming as Sparrow in Mother Goose.
Presto, we have a whodunit, a wonderland of intrigue where both
Courage and Cowardice can dramatize themselves. Snodgrass's

The Death of Cock Robin is a fine tour de force, not just a literary stunt, for it is really more of a reverie upon the original rather than a deconstruction or subversion of it. Indeed, his book—thick with historical implication and literary allusion, bilingual puns, acrostics, anagrams—seems not to have been written so much under the agony of influence as under a fully conscious joy of it: Joyce, Kafka, Dostoevsky, Shakespeare, the Bible, the Latin Mass, Lewis Carroll, Edward Lear, Freud, e. e. cummings, T. S. Eliot, Wallace Stevens, and a host of the less obvious. What Snodgrass has given us, among other things, is a great modernist nursery rhyme, wordy playground cunningly designed for literate adults to romp in, adults who, nurtured on modern classics, were once, as Joyce put it in *Finnegans Wake,* "jung and easily freudened."

The moderns had more than a passing interest in levels of awareness; so too Snodgrass. The psychological dimension of *The Death of Cock Robin* is archetypal, involving initiation, progress, and attempts at escape from egocentrism. It is reminiscent of the identity-threatening adventures of Alice in *Through the Looking Glass* in some ways. There is, for one thing, a sense of entanglement and narcissistic doubling from which W. D., like Alice, must escape. In both, as well, we have the world of dream, a major difference being that the Alice books are framed narratives where we start with a familiar quotidian and move into the dream world of infantile fears. In *Cock Robin,* we never see a verisimilar world; it exists only by suggestion and allusion beyond the continuous dream or nightmare. In any event, the realms we enter in Snodgrass verge, as in Carroll, on the dream state: stasis (reinforced by DeLoss McGraw's strange, floating figures—color images vaguely reminiscent of the painted dreams of Marc Chagall), absence of time, rerun scenes, levitation, incoherence of space, inconsequence, the irrational, nonsense phrases, disproportion, indifference to suffering and death, inverted justice, and police-state terror.

As to psychodrama and developmental progress, we don't, in *Cock Robin,* have the infantile Tweedles or Humpty Dumpty to symbolize former narcissistic selves transcended, but rather W. D., a narrative persona moving toward self-transcendence and self-preservation. The central theme in *Cock Robin* is a reitera-

tion and elaboration of a theme that has haunted Snodgrass from
his very first book: the artist's bloody struggle to survive in the
large world of society and in its smaller Darwinian reflection,
the groves of academe. *Heart's Needle* is full of "enemies and
rivals" ("A Cardinal") and is about survival in a world hostile
to art. Poems like "The Operation" make it clear the poet is a
dangerous person, someone to be neutralized or neutered ("a
bright straight razor / Inched on my stomach down my groin, /
Paring the brown hair off') and while he lies a-bed in a post-op
druggy fog, outside the hospital room "sirens may / Wail for the
fugitive." The world of this first book features a number of real
and imaginary prisons. "A Cardinal" attacks other artists who
"praise what it pays to praise / praise soap and garbage cans, /
joining with the majority / in praising man-eat-man . . ." In other
poems academics are the targets—the world of ivory towerism
("The Campus on the Hill") and careerism ("April Inventory")
where intellectual and political fads reign, and "one by one the
solid scholars / Get the degrees, the jobs, the dollars." Snodgrass
has always insisted that many literary scholars fail because
beauty, mystery, gentleness fall beyond the purview of their studies, because they are long on theory and short on humanity. At
the close of "April Inventory," he affirms what the basis of his
survival will be:

> There is a value underneath
> The gold and silver in my teeth.
>
> .   .   .   .
>
> There is a gentleness survives
> That will outspeak and has its reasons.
> There is a loveliness exists,
> Preserves us, not for specialists.

Cut to the poet thirty years later. The situation worsens, the
plot sickens, loveliness languishes, and haters of various plumes
and stripes are after Cock Robin and W. D. One of DeLoss
McGraw's color images is entitled "The Poet Ridiculed By Hysterical Academics." But ridicule is a minor worry, and W. D.
must face more dangerous foes, must overcome a paralyzing fear,
which he shows signs of doing even early in the sequence: "W. D.
is Concerned about the Character Assassination of Cock Robin."

But, at this point in the narrative, W. D. does little but register a frightening situation made worse by friends who selfishly want to know nothing of the evil that spreads like a plague in their claustral world. The communal refrain is "Yo no quiero verla; / Yo no lo se." W. D., on the other hand, is fully conscious of the horrifying reality of "secret inspectors" and realizes the fatal political and personal consequences of general cowardice and self-interest:

> As your stock falls, old friends
>   Fall off. Fall into danger—
> If you survive depends
>   On some total stranger.
>
>   .   .   .   .
>
> All you once knew goes strange.
>   Some you've known all their lives
> Outside your window range,
>   Tongues flashing slick as knives . . . .

Such a situation touches off in the reader a powerful sense of historical déjà vu: witch hunts, Gestapo roundups, the McCarthy era, Argentinian death squads, Franco and the murder of Garcia Lorca, the KGB and the disappearance of Isaac Babel, the gulagging of Osip Mandelstam and Anna Akhmatova, to name just a few.

In "Interrogation" one of Snodgrass's most powerful inversions, not only of Mother Goose but of an entire elegiac tradition, is realized in the aftermath of the killing. The elegy throughout literary history has usually made use of the pathetic fallacy and featured, with greater or lesser degrees of subtlety, winds, woods, skies, and animals sympathetically responding to the death of the person who has occasioned the lament. So too in the Mother Goose original—all of Nature mourns, and a host of birds, a beetle, a fish, and even a bull participate in honoring Cock Robin's memory with a procession and solemn graveside service. In *Cock Robin*, however, Cock Robin is an outlaw ("His Cockiness whose Robinhood / Echoes the Forest of Sure Would") and the pervasive atmosphere of this dream world is fear, fear of guilt by association. To the question of who will dig his grave, we hear: "I'm committed, says the mole, / To exploring my own hole . . ."

To the question of who will bear the casket: "Count me out there, says the ant. / I'm too small, I simply can't." And so on, until:

> All the beasts of earth and air
> Fell a-weaslin' and a-bobbin'
> When they heard of the death
> Of poor Cock Robin.

In another poem in the sequence—"W. D., without Disguise, Is Recognized by the Dark Comedian but Denies His Relationship with Cock Robin"—Snodgrass implicates W. D. in the general fear that prompts disassociation and denial, subtly linking him with St. Peter's denial of Christ:

> "Then you were not his follower?"
>   . . . .
> I stonewalled like a rock, came through
> Unscathed, yet only said what's true.
> I made them all look bad, then flew
> Their coop. What kind of bird just crew?

He simultaneously links him, however, to political villains with the verb *stonewalled*, this coined during the Watergate hearings when many of Nixon's henchmen stalled, resisted, and double-talked in order to avoid telling the truth. Thus, W. D., in not telling the truth, would seem to deal in the kind of deception and self-betrayal we attribute to Mr. Evil, but Snodgrass intends this, for Mr. Evil is to some extent, in "Cock Robin's Roost," a shaped poem with *en face* reflection, an alter ego. Here Mr. Evil says: "Many a man condemns me, and some / Are far more like me than they know." This is a profound, necessary, but perhaps unwelcome truth—that we all incorporate part of the dark adversarial Other within the self.

Which brings me to a consideration of the shadowy "W. D." One of the compelling fruits of Snodgrass's reimagining of Mother Goose is the invention of the character of W. D. In only a few poems in the sequence, we have either an objective narrator or Snodgrass in propria persona, but most often, like Eliot (Prufrock) and Berryman (Henry), or Conrad (Marlow) and Fitzgerald (Carraway), Snodgrass makes good modernist use of W. D. (not so coincidentally named) as a distancing device, a character who is both a friend to Cock Robin and his psychological double. W. D. is also the archetypal Ishmael who survives to tell the cautionary tale. Often we wonder to what extent Nick Carraway is Fitzgerald, or Prufrock, Eliot, but with "W. D." we have creation ex nihilo, for we need only, ahem, compare DeLoss McGraw's unlikely renderings of "W. D." with those dustjacket photos of W. D. Snodgrass, he of the magnificent Dostoevskian whiskers, to know there is absolutely no resemblance. The narrative persona, at the outset, admits that he searches his memory for Cock Robin in "my brain's ingrown thicket. . . ." The whole narrative, too, follows a modernist paradigm suggested by Eliot in "The Dry Salvages": "we had the experience but missed the meaning." This is a structural strategy we find in *The Great Gatsby*, *The Heart of Darkness*, and even more recently in *Humbolt's Gift* in which recovery of meaning, self-forgiveness, and exorcism, among other things, are at stake. In novels like these, we often have writers looking into a mirror and Snodgrass's playful strategy in *Cock Robin* is similar. In one title, for example, we learn that "W. D. Searches for Cock Robin in the Weave of his Thought." In another, "W. D. Becomes Entangled in the Nest of His Thought," W. D. compares the process of reflection to being in some

> Hall of Mirrors where
> each thought invokes its
> counterthought, each
> desire its
> antipathy, where all is
> double and that double
> doubled . . .
>
> .   .   .   .   .
>
>   until
> you meet your own self
> coming out the other side and,
> unsure of welcome, hold
> your hand out to inquire:
> Cock Robin, i presume?

W. D., like his creator, is drawn to the drama of Cock Robin because of his own interest in song. In the "W. D.'s Blues," he sings, "Gonna keep one feather, 'case I ever write a song." In the

same poem, he also defines the nature and function of song:
"Gonna fly Cock Robin's feather like a bright kite in the sky; /
Run it up my flag pole just to keep my spirits high." Like Snodgrass his creator, W. D. himself is an aspiring creator of song,
inspired by the heroic model of Cock Robin. But unlike Cock
Robin who is too visible, too fatally flashy, W. D. will learn in
the final poems of the book that survival in a society hostile to
art means camouflage, disguise, and ingenious means of escape,
or as Stephen Dedalus before him learned: silence, exile, and
cunning. (This has been at the very heart of much of Snodgrass's
work from early *Heart's Needle* poems such as "A Cardinal,"
"Papageno," "Song," "Orpheus," and "April Inventory.") Like
Dedalus, his commonsensical artist predecessor, W. D. goes to
the air in "Assuming Fine Feathers, W. D. Takes Flight":

> Hot on my track still,
>   But I tricked 'em;
> Now who's your criminal;
>   Where's your victim?
>   *Dee-flee-a-beadle-tweedle-free!*

In Snodgrass's reimagining, it might be impossible to answer the
question of who killed Cock Robin, but it is not at all difficult
to understand why he was killed. For all of the playfulness and
sheer fun of the book, it is typically modernist in its deep moral
and aesthetic concerns, concerns which are virtually insepa-
rable. From the book's beginning, in "The Charges against Cock
Robin," Snodgrass describes a Kulturkampf that is always contemporary. That the conflict is deadly and based on difference
is emphasized ironically by the judge, "His Honor James T. 'Just
call me Jim' Crowe" who reads the indictment, with comic vox
populi ejaculations that are funnier for also being parodic of
Greek choral responses:

> It is charged he's been known to warble
>   (*Deplorable!*)
> An aria, a love song, or recitatif
>   (*Good Grief!*)
> When he goes walking, long after curfew
>   (*Lord Preserve you!*)
> Waking up both town and country.
>   (*What effrontery!*)

We find it far more injurious
(We're just furious!)
That he sings beyond other bird's range
(He's strange!)
Though they practice and pay the best teachers
(Poor creatures!)
While his tunes baffle us and defeat us.
(Elitist!)

The list of charges goes on to accuse Cock Robin of dressing in a fashion "neither generic nor respectable." The other birds want him to get *"expectable."* His clothing of "bright shreds and patches" offends them. They would have him get *"a uniform."* Further, these "birds of one stripe" warn him to both *"Be our type!"* and *"Get duller!"*. The "or else" is clearly implied. It is important to note that *The Death of Cock Robin* begins with a courtroom setting to remind us of the full power of the state that is brought against this solitary but dangerous singer. And the state of the State is nicely suggested by one word that describes and calls to mind many politically oppressive regimes, "curfew."

As I said earlier, it is difficult for the modernist to separate aesthetics and political repression, and in "W. D. Tries to Warn Cock Robin," Snodgrass builds a wildly comic indictment that underscores the truth of André Malraux's brilliant observation: "Le mauvais goût mène aux crimes." One of the first crimes of bad taste Snodgrass points to is censorship in the name of morality:

The Brutish are coming, the Brutish;
The Rude-Coats with snares and bum-drumming!
    The Skittish and Prudish
    The Brattish and Crude
    Who'll check on your morals
    And find your song's lewd
Then strip off the bay leaves and laurels
That garnished your brows and your food.
All tongues and all tastebuds benumbing,
    They'll dull all your senses
    Then lull your defenses
And rule you through blue-nosed and tasteless pretenses;
    The Brutish!

Next, W. D. warns that the "Ruffians are coming." Not the Russians of the well-known comic film, but "Pan-Slobs from Vulgaria" who will "stomp out your stuffings." If you're caught "Knowing more than your own name; they'll bury you." These violent "red-necked invaders," in Snodgrass's view, are as much a threat to civilization as was Khruschev of the atomic Cold War. The next two stanzas concern the threat posed by super-patriotic "Merkans," nationalistic jingos, who'll blind you with "terms periphrastic" and fanatical "Krishans" who'll keep you from seeing clearly with "visions / Of undying blisses." The Krishans will "double-cross you with kisses / and blessings." So far the satire against political and religious despotism has been Popian, but it turns Swiftian with the "Youmans." Wordplay and punning keep at bay any tone of savage indignation, but the Youmans are still seen as dangerously violent and self-destructive, if in blackly comical terms:

> The Youmans are coming; the Youmans
> Hear the backslapping rascals, the chumming
>> Of Masculs and Woomans
>> Who built up this Babel
>> Of Atoms and Evils
>> And hope that they're able
> To raise further cain and upheavals.
> That Garden foreclosed in the fable
> Foretold how this world's going slumming:
>> In cold greed, the cowards
>> Still split and unite
>> For unneeded powers,
>> While backbiting spite
>> Pulls down all their towers;
>> With air, sea and soil
>> And their own minds to spoil
> And spin their bright cosmos to unending night;
>> The Youmans!

The Youmans indeed! The progress of the stanza skillfully fades its humor at line seven and thereafter slowly wipes the smile from our faces. The prophetic echoes merge into a trio of words that by themselves carry a political and environmental charge, but the rhyme word *spoil* in the next line clobbers the reader. Throughout the book we often have a wonderful comic entertainment upset by the introduction of dreadful reminders of secret police, interrogations, and torture—all before a backdrop of infinity, nothingness, and death. The use of an odd mixture of comedy and terror is a strategy that Snodgrass pursues throughout to keep the reader's expectation unsettled.

The works of such modernist writers as Joyce, Eliot, Pound, Nabokov, and Faulkner are often described as being difficult because of the range of allusion these writers display, and because of the pressure they exert on language itself, often demanding of a reader an extensive vocabulary in his own language as well as knowledge of classical or modern foreign languages. So too with Snodgrass, as in the way he satirizes human folly. "Homo nonsapiens conturbat me" is one of the refrains in "Assuming Fine Feathers, W. D. Takes Flight," one which calls to mind Psalm 43 from the Ordinary of the Latin Mass where the psalmist says: "I will praise Thee upon a harp, O God, my God: why art thou sad, O my soul?" ["Confitebor tibi in cithara, Deus, Deus meus: quare tristis es, anima mea, et quare conturbas me?"]. Wittily theological, the Snodgrassian soul answers that what it finds disturbing is the lack of wisdom in human beings: "Homo nonsapiens conturbat me." W. D., like Cock Robin, also "sings beyond the other bird's range," beyond our national eighth-grade reading level, thereby revealing tastes that are dangerously undemocratic if not unpatriotic. Malraux's notion about bad taste leading to crime means, in this case, crime against an individual who possesses knowledge and good taste.

Undemocratic taste, the association of censorship and social tyranny with bad taste or pop culture is again sounded in "W. D. Meets Mr. Evil While Removing the Record of Bartók and Replacing it with a Recent Recording by the Everly Brothers in Order to Create a Mood Conducive to Search for Cock Robin." Mr. Evil tells W. D. that he wants to find what is "on your mind." Only Thought Police can keep such a political state in power. Like the Nazis, especially Dr. Joseph Goebbels, minister of propaganda, whose chilling portrait Snodgrass has unforgettably rendered in The Fuehrer Bunker, Mr. Evil would cleanse the arts of "degenerate" influences like Bartók. These "grim sounds" must give way to "hopeful tunes, loving and cheerful." Down with cultural elitism, bring on the Everly Brothers with a

Psalm of unchanging Brotherhood,
Fake chords real folks would like real good,
Cut platters of pattering platitudes
To impart the politic, pat attitudes
Taught by our founder, Dr. Garbles,
Who struck dumb multitudes with marbles

Held in mouthfuls of popular melody.
Or better still, this high fidelity
Digital of an eighteen-minute
Gap: you'll feel, each time you spin it,
Pure as a Quaker, freed from violence
And expletives by blissful silence.

The author of *The Fuehrer Bunker* knows well the cynical mentality and brownshirt behavior that cheerleads book-burning not only in Berlin but in West Virginia, or removes *Huckleberry Finn* from high school libraries and reading lists. If Goebbels, as he is said to have said, felt like reaching for a revolver every time he heard the word "culture," could not the same be said of Nixon, Spiro T. Agnew, and many of their cohorts? Wasn't it Agnew, or William Safire, or someone from the stable of ghostwriters who gave us the phrase "effete intellectual snobs"? And the Bush White House which first gave us "spin doctors" and "spin control"? "Dr. Garbles" is an effective allusion, significantly connected to the famous eighteen-minute Nixonian gap—the attempt at control that failed, failed to suppress information about the greatest abuse of power in American political history. In such a political environment, it is easy to appreciate the kind of danger Snodgrass has in mind for a singer like Cock Robin, easy to imagine the kind of pressure felt, at various times, by singers like Robert Lowell, Daniel Berrigan, Boris Pasternak, García Lorca, Osip Mandelstam, and others.

It is clear, therefore, why Snodgrass indicts a sensibility that prefers only verse of easy access, transparent poems that never need a second reading, that never call attention to their own artificiality. What he himself has produced and continues to produce is informed by a diametrically opposite sensibility, a modernist sensibility whose verbal structure never allows a reader to forget the knowledge, craft, and ingenuity that go into the creation of such a well-wrought urn. This has always been a hallmark of Snodgrass's poetry.

Another characteristic of *Cock Robin* and his other work is a
sympathy for the abyss. Existentialism may no longer be in
vogue, but this doesn't mean that the absurd, nothingness, or the
black holes of daily existence have vanished. Nor does it mean
that the values of solidarity and choice, or the themes of evil,
guilt, and hope dramatized by writers Snodgrass mentions or
alludes to (Camus, Kafka, and Dostoevsky) no longer matter.
They clearly matter to Snodgrass. Into the dark claustral world
of betrayal and cowardice, of bondage in the "land of Gyp and
Be Gypped" where most birds belong to the repellent species
identified by H. L. Mencken over fifty years ago (*boobus ameri-
canus*), the poet adumbrates several kinds of hope and courage.
When Cock Robin is on the lam, hunted by inspectors and secret
police, when "the sky's unsettled" and "hawkwinged shadows"
appear, he is taken in by the "Storm Family" and given large
doses of nonpossessive love of the unconditional variety:

> We won't ask your opinions
> While you roost in our dominions;
>   They're your own and we simply don't care.
> We won't ask you what your father does
> 'Cause things like that don't bother us
>   On the heights of an old kitchen chair.
>   .   .   .   .
>
> All your fancier emotions
> Fall someplace outside our notions;
> .   .   .   .
> We can't drive away your inner storm
> But we'll keep your bed and dinner warm
>   And help talk away a nightmare;
> So in case you get a weeping jag
> Come creep inside our sleeping bag
>   Tucked up on an old kitchen chair.
>   Milk that's spilt
>   Blame and guilt
>   And a cold sense of wrong in the air
>   Sometimes wilt
>   In a quilt
> Wrapped up snug on an old kitchen chair.

The speaker—some member of the Storm Family—hopes in the
final stanza for better weather, sunny air filled with birds and

the sound of bees, an air filled "with zephyrs / And the fields with lambs and heifers," weather that will launch Cock Robin "from that old kitchen chair" simply "Cause we care / How you fare" when "far from our old kitchen chair." There is a bracing homeyness, normalcy, and sense of love that the "Anthem of the Storm Family" exudes; it reminds me of John Cheever's wonderful notion that "sanctuary is the essence of love." In protecting Cock Robin, The Storm Family also reminds us of the rare European Christians of the 1940s who sheltered fugitive Jews. This poem is a deeply moving testament to friendship and solidarity, a fine defiance of the existential abyss.

At the outset of this essay, I mentioned the elegy. Built into the traditional elegy is some notion of hope and solace, some kind of consolation or compensation for loss, but the closer we come to the twenty-first century, the more the possibility of conventional consolation becomes tenuous because of the disappearance of traditional religious belief. In our time, for many people, song that is a reminder of the possibility of tenderness and beauty is itself consolation enough, and it is this kind of solace that makes itself felt in five closing poems of *The Death of Cock Robin*. These poems chart W. D.'s escape from bondage in the land of "Be Gypped" into the promised land of song. Here, however, it is important that "land" not be confused with external "place," for place in this book is really unimportant, unimportant because there is no place to go. The locale and theater of activity in the entire book is the mind and, as Milton put it in *Paradise Lost*, "The mind is its own place, and in itself, / Can make a heaven of hell, a hell of heaven." The narrative's vertical progress toward song and celebration is finally a rejection of the terrifying underside of human consciousness, a victory over dark powers. The only important journey is inward, and W. D.'s journey is one of experience into the holy self where godhead resides. Like Daedalus, W. D. ultimately plots a feathery escape, and finds, as he implicitly predicted early in the sequence, a way "To overcome brute force and mightiness; Getting things off the ground takes flightiness" ("W. D. Lifts Ten Times the Weight Of His Own Body"). But the real launchpad for W. D.'s escape is "Credo" with its affirmative repetitions based upon "The House That Jack Built":

Here is the void, the blank, black eye
That watches pink putti dogfight the sky
To harry dark angels that fly high to spy
While old Mr. Evil's still telling his lie,
And on creeps the rumor, sinuous, sly,
Like worms into hiding or some unknown pest
That could riddle the 8-storey towering nest
Battered by breezes from east and from west,
Empowering the breath, forthright and strong,
That saved so long from rot and from wrong
The lifelong, lovesprung, airborne song
Cock Robin sung.

The sense of *de profundis*, of a prophetic voice crying from the belly of the beast, deepens and intensifies with each stanza as the poet, like Carpenter Jack, goes a-building his deeply convincing structure. Cock Robin's song simultaneously acknowledges "the void," "the dark angels," "Mr. Evil," and his "lie" while providing a refuge from them. In fact, the implication is that the song would matter little without some adversarial relationship with darkness and absurdity. There is a necessary and complementary relationship between good and evil; one cannot exist meaningfully without the other. The song might not change the world or make much happen, but it can change one's attitude toward a world that is beautifully ambiguous.

In the next poem, "W. D. Creates a Device for Escaping," Snodgrass presents us with the image and symbol of a wheel while describing a one-step-at-a-time progress that involves "A con foot, then a pro foot," and "A joy foot, then a woe foot":

Or turn weak like old Sisyface,
Letting him roll back to the base;
A yes foot, then a no foot.

"Sisyface" resonates with both the classical and the modern. One thinks of the moving closure of Camus's essay defining rebellion, hope, the absurd and, especially, absurd creation—the last two sentences of "Le mythe de Sisyphe": "La lutte elle-même vers les sommets suffit à remplir le coeur d'homme. Il faut imaginer Sisyphe heureux." *La lutte*—the struggle or the battle is often an inward one, and that is especially true of *The Death of Cock Robin*, with its dreamlike qualities and its focus on problems of the soul, and the effects of song on the soul. We have to imagine the songster happy in his circular struggle with self and the extra-mental world. In the penultimate poem, "W. D. Disguised as Cock Robin and Hidden Deep in Crimson," Snodgrass writes:

> I dopplegang some grander
> Land that schizophrenics
> Colonize from earth,
> One with the salamander,
> With that flaming phoenix
> Or lodgepole pine whose clenched cones need
> The forest fire to cast their seed.

Walt Whitman's open road might eventually lead to attempts at happiness on other planets, but those attempts can only be doomed. There will always be real enemies beyond the perceiving self, but the disease implied in this last stanza is psychological at root, and the "seed," wherever it is cast, will only sprout "Youmans." The suggestion here seems to be that hope and happiness must come, if they are to come at all, from within. Or, as John Logan, one of Snodgrass's generation, puts it beautifully in another context, "Only the dreamer can change the dream."

The Spectacles of Wit in W. D. Snodgrass's Recent Poetry

Philip Raisor

SOME CRITICS, LOOKING TO PUT A PIN IN THAT CHAP, SEE W. D. SNOD-
grass in his world as a Joycean-like creator who evolves from
lyric to dramatic, finally arriving in his handiwork as "invisible,
refined out of existence, indifferent, paring his fingernails."
Others find him in our world, quite visible, walking through the
universe, attentive, adjusting his spectacles. Snodgrass must be
pleased with the discord. In his 1975 collection of critical essays
and lectures, *In Radical Pursuit*,[1] he establishes that he does not
want to be defined by his work, anymore, he says, than Shakespeare is: "We cannot sum up Shakespeare; we can only set up
housekeeping there." Nor does he want the world summed up.
He finds that the Symbolists tried, and that they "cut down on
the terrible disparity and incongruity of our world." Snodgrass
sees himself—detached and attached, impersonal and confessional—in a world which is not fixed and which is full of contra-
dictory multitudes. "Yes" is the poet's word Snodgrass says in
his recent "A Darkling Alphabet," and "breadth" is the poet's
aim. It cannot be otherwise, he feels, because "We cannot know
the qualities of our world apart from the qualities of ourselves
who perceive it."[2] The universe is imagined and relative. Housekeeping for us all is the same. We cannot find the Truth, only
our own.

In this world of becoming, therefore, the world outside of us
and the world within are both dependent upon our powers of
invention. The problem with "hysterical academics" for Snodgrass is that they have such limited powers—single-eyed, con-
strictive, judgmental. Shakespeare, Bruno, and Montaigne had
broader powers, he says. They moved "in a world of limitless
change, of rolling and flowing, boundaries shifting and re-

43

forming, realities dissolving and illusions becoming real." Snod-
grass sees invention as an intellectual pleasure, one which, as
Arnold Stein defines it, is more Elizabethan than contemporary.
For the Renaissance, says Stein,

> *Invention* was an important word, and could stand for the power of
> a man's mind to conceive, to see likeness and unlikeness—not
> merely with an earnest, literal, separative logic, but with the vir-
> tuoso's ability to forgo straight performance, and to mix his cate-
> gories, while he displays his imaginative skill by the conscious
> control of what he is doing and by the surprising new lights he opens
> on his subject. *Invention* also signified the power to recognize the
> possibilities of a subject and to develop them, to bring out the laten-
> cies of a theme while observing the rules, written and unwritten, of
> propriety, tact, and grace. Mock encomia, false arguments, paradoxes
> and problems—these were not only part of the student's authorized
> pleasure in maintaining outrageous propositions, but they were by
> no means beneath the dignity of mature talent. The standard tech-
> niques by which a theme was elevated or depressed, amplified or
> compressed—in the hands of a master were more than techniques;
> they were a mark of quality of mind.[3]

This is *Wit*, as the Renaissance understood it, and the quality of
mind which for Snodgrass makes Shakespeare so "bafflingly
great . . . , the drive toward variousness, toward turbulent diversity, in that violent mixing of genres which so disturbed conti-
nental critics; realistic scenes collide with highly fanciful
stylized scenes; prose rubs shoulders with blank verse or even
with tight rhyme; high wit mixes with buffoonery, high tragedy
with melodrama . . . All conventions are seized on; none is admitted to yield final truth."

If we think of Snodgrass's own oeuvre as a play, then from his
early verse at the University of Iowa to the present, his art is
truly "tragical-comical-historical-pastoral," mixing "confessional" poems, nonsense verse, "historical" monologues, dirty
limericks, early songs, dance suites, sonata and aria forms, free
verse, nonce and traditional patterns. This same drive for variousness is evident, to some extent, in many of the individual
works. Critics who see only a hodgepodge of styles miss Snodgrass's point: "Multiplicity, density, and variousness" is the "way
our world feels, the way our mind is." *In Heart's Needle* lofty

sonnets mingle with slangy free verse, while the Furies and Underworld Powers hover near "Riots in Algeria, in Cypress, in Alabama"; in *After Experience* lyric poems, poems about paintings, and translations reflect a multidimensional world; in *The Fuehrer Bunker* monologues and poly-voiced forms explore multiple layers of consciousness; in *W. D.'s Midnight Carnival* and *The Death of Cock Robin* dialogues between poems and paintings examine an ever-expanding space. Even when Snodgrass himself thinks of separating forms, content, and voices he tends not to. Seeing his lighter pieces as a relief from his more somber efforts, he has said, "When I can no longer stand the horrific evils of the Third Reich—and the continuing shock of finding them not so unlike other governments, other people, I have known—I turn to the troubadours." Certainly the patient Sir Pilgrim (in *Six Troubadour Songs*) who mutely withstands the testing tortures of two amorous ladies is not Hitler gnawing on millions; but when both whine about betrayal, they come from the same kennel. In a recent interview, Snodgrass acknowledges that *The Death of Cock Robin* is in the lighter vein, playful and "meant to dazzle and razzledazzle."[4] He does say, also, "I was thinking, I confess, when I was writing the Cock Robin poems about the very bad reception I got from people for *The Fuehrer Bunker*." And upon further reflection he adds "Come to think of it, the Cock Robin poems do get into really difficult and painful problems from time to time." I do not doubt that Snodgrass works on different forms at different times to release his mind and energies in different ways, but his observation on the oppositional elements in the current work reflects a thought process even more central to his practice.

Snodgrass's recent collaboration with the painter DeLoss McGraw is clearly an extension of this pluralistic outlook and the fulfillment of an art form which he envisaged much earlier. Even as *Heart's Needle* (along with Robert Lowell's *Life Studies*) was launching the Confessional movement, Snodgrass, in a 1960 lecture, was looking past the present. He was saying that after the symbolists, the modernists, and the "place-centered" poets (of whom he was one), a new space-age poetry would develop. This poetry, he said, "would create a vision of ourselves as dancers in endless space, finite dancers in a space not infinite but undefined." Snodgrass remained place-centered through the 60s and 70s, but was responsive when McGraw brought to him what he had long sought in his own imagination, "an art form of objects and intelligences positioned in space and relative only to each other." McGraw's paintings were archetypal rather than impressionistic or realistic, and Snodgrass saw a new way to explore those serious problems of self and world which were embodied in his thinking.

This collaboration is firmly established in, what Jean H. Hagstrum terms, the "pictorialist tradition of Western culture,"[5] that association which from Horace and Simonides to the present yoked together the sister arts of poetry and painting. Snodgrass's earliest ventures into *ut pictura poesis* included the addition of Paul Klee's illustrations with his (and Lore Segal's) translations of Christian Morgenstern's *Gallows Songs* and the poetic interpretations of five postimpressionist painters in *After Experience*. But the Snodgrass/McGraw union goes beyond the emblem book relationship in which the painting is a pendant for the poem, or the poem is a verbal equivalent of the painting, to a more intense interpenetration of the two arts. The result is a unique extension of the "curious perspective" tradition which Ernest B. Gilman illuminates in his fine study *The Curious Perspective: Literary and Pictorial Wit in the Seventeenth Century.* Using tricks of perspective—mirrors, lenses, telescopes—visual artists achieved ingenious effects by manipulating linear perspectives. Analogously, seventeenth-century English poets used allegory, personification, metaphor, and various forms of wordplay to achieve similar ends. Says Gilman, "The curious perspective violates the ordered perfection of pictorial space as verbal wit violates the expository clarity of language. Both exploit the witness's uncertainty in the presence of duplicitous images but repay his puzzlement with . . . a sudden apprehension of meanings beyond the geometer's grasp."[6] Snodgrass has long varied his angles of vision. For example, he has focused the single, reflective light of the ward nurse on the self ("These Trees Stand . . ."), viewed reality through the mirrored window of Adolph Eichmann ("A Visitation"), as well as the prisms of the bunkered Nazis, adjusted the invented spectacles of Morgenstern's Korf to collect and see all through the world's texts ("The Spectacles"), and developed a Hall of Mirrors which, in *The Death of Cock Robin*, is like W. D.'s mind "where / each thought evokes its / counter-thought, each/ desire its / antipathy, where all is / double and that double/ doubled. . . ." Weaned on the Metaphysical poets, Bernini's baroque style, and Renaissance plays and songs, Snodgrass still exploits his mentors' worlds. With McGraw he expands a parallactic art into an even broader text of multiple meanings.

In *W. D.'s Midnight Carnival*,[7] a collection of fifteen poems and eighteen paintings, McGraw's titles (e.g., "W. D.'s House of Horrors," "W. D., The Human Torch," "W. D. Sings a Song about Skulls and Flowers") emphasize the voice and trials of a persona. Snodgrass, responding to or initiating McGraw's gouaches, often directs our attention to a broader world (e.g., "House of Horrors," "Human Torch," "A Strolling Minstrel's Ballad of the Skulls and Flowers"). The titling is characteristic of a design that draws us into an expanding and ever-changing universe which engages both our senses and imaginations, particular emotions and universal truths, contemporary events and mythological constructs. W. D. is as many-figured as Leopold Bloom in Nighttown and accompanied by as many hybrid spectres. In fact, on one level, this "carnival" is a story of W. D.'s day, beginning with "Sideshow—Mr. Sun" (which Snodgrass titles "The Capture of Mr. Sun") and ending with the sideshow that both McGraw and Snodgrass title "The Capture of Mr. Moon." Sun and moon bracket the trials of W. D. (a high-wire walker, a human torch, a tattooed man, a drunken minstrel), who lives in a world "just like what it is"—a house of horrors and a hall of mirrors.

In this world each scene suggests endless space and a finite problem. For example, McGraw's tenth painting in the series is titled "W. D. Shields Himself". This watercolor gouache-collage is a starkly framed black background, dominated by a multicolored comic mask held firmly by W. D. But the subtlety of design and hue extend our attention to the discords inherent in the scene. The mask is part moon smiling and part sun threatening, its spikes assaulting the vulnerable figure. In the guise of clown and with weapons of humor, W. D. shields himself from the all-absorbing thrust of nature's darkness, but in the process is diminished by his defensive role. The scene is both comic and sinister, suggesting that disguise is as dangerous to the self as is a mysterious and constricted universe.

Snodgrass responds to the tensions in the painting by developing a polyvoiced poem in which discord, also, is central:

DR. P.H.D. DARK, HYPNOTIST

Engrossing as a black hole
on your TV screen, I send out
no powers; I accept all
energies, all joys and juices . . .

    1, 2, 3, 4, 5,
    Are your loves alive?

My cone of eclipse, this wizard's
peaked black dunce cap slips
down on your brow, the brain's
drained batteries consent . . .

    6, 7, 8, 9, 10,
    Hope for what and when?

Cold be no more than
heat loss, wanting warmth,
dark be but only
light's lack, locked affections . . .

    9, 8, 7, 6, 5,
    Do numbed nerves survive?

Evil by default of good,
forfeit or shortfall, be. I am
your mentor, priest, your lover.
You cannot open your eyes.

    4, 3, 2, 1, 0,
    Will you waken? No.

One voice, Dr. Dark's, oppressive and restrictive (one of Snodgrass's "hysterical academics"), is equated with death and its attendant mask. It is death-in-life obliterating the brain's distinctions and driving home the nihility of all things. The other voice is childlike and inquisitive, breaking into Dr. Dark's monologue. It is the energy of "joys and juices" and the rhymes and rhythms that rise and fall in the darkness. It is life-in-death, with no

W. D. Shields Himself, 40″ × 30″ w/c-gouache-collage

W. D.'s Midnight Carnival Friends, 30" × 40" w/c-gouache-collage

illusions about life-after-death. Once brain-dead or physically dead "Will you awaken? No."

Together, both painting and poem explore the possibilities of and consequences to the exposed and self-contained life and the manifold threats to its extinction. But while McGraw emphasizes the ambivalence of W. D.'s condition, Snodgrass explores the psychological and moral choices inherent in it. In effect the juxtaposition of painting and poem constitutes an extended metaphor running on two tracks of meaning (visual and verbal) that leave irreconcilables unyoked. This is characteristic of the collaboration, though the degree of differences vary. McGraw and Snodgrass may agree that the "Human Torch" is a fascinating art-for-art's-sake poet and the "25¢ Song" is the archetypal elevator music, but the gouache that McGraw titles "W. D. Before Puberty" and the "Carnival Is a Clear Mirror of Chromium" which Snodgrass retitles "The Hall of Mirrors" is not for both a child-like, glittering "jovial hullabaloo among the spheres," and the "tattooed man" that for McGraw is a wonder-to-behold is, for Snodgrass, a solipsistic complainer. The dialogue is persistent and fertile, confronting us with enigmas, double-visions, unresolved meanings, and, of course, the "openness" inherent in their practices and aims.

In typical "curious perspective" manner, however, the Snodgrass/McGraw collaboration directs us not only toward the "midnight" problems in this extended space, but also the "carnival" aspects, preserving a tension between the two. W. D.'s Midnight Carnival, in its deliberately fantastic and unrealistic mode and in its overall structure, combines epiphanic scenes and witty poems into a masque, which if not as elaborate as those produced by Ben Jonson and Inigo Jones is nonetheless a celebratory spectacle of music, dance, scenery, and words. Its audience, of course, is not courtly lords and ladies; therefore it takes liberties with character and style. For Jonson, Lady Mary Wroth, to whom he dedicates The Alchemist, becomes a prototype for the nymphs in his The Masque of Blackness, who are the epitome of womanly virtue:

> Madame, had all antiquitie beene lost,
> All historie seal'd up, and fables crost;
> That we had left us, nor by time, nor place

Least mention of a *Nymph*, a *Muse*, a *Grace*.
But even their names were to be made a-new,
Who could not but create them all, from you?[8]

McGraw's Carnival Girl, deftly coiffured and richly costumed, who darkly attracts W. D. is wittily turned by Snodgrass into a mythological nymph whose "virtues" he expands for his taste and our times:

O she does teach the torches to burn bright
    As a rich Jewel in an Ethiop's ear,
            Romeo,
            Romeo,
        Ro' me o-ver
        In the clover
        .   .   .   .
    And would her mother let her out?
Even as a common Italian young woman
Loaned her fresh visage to the holy mysteries,
So here, St. Anne, who's next to the Madonna,
    And then? And then? And then?
A glove, that I might touch that cheek
            Ham and eggs
            Between your legs;
        Mine's got meat with gravy.

This revel of gaudy colors, costumed figures, slang, wisecracks, and whimsical allusiveness provides a rich texture for a series of rotating and tractable panels. Preserving the masques' allegorical import, *Midnight Carnival* features a nondramatic movement which contains the usual sun god descending and horned moon rising as well as an antimasque of pygmies, satyrs, and giants. In the seventeenth-century masques, as Robert M. Adams notes, "the whole structure led toward the presentation of the supreme compliment to the most important person present. And then the audience was called on to mingle with the masquers. . . . The final dance circled around the central luminary of the occasion, everyone took part in it because no one was present who was not part of the court, and everyone in the court was bound, by ties of loyalty and reverence, to its supreme figure."[9] In the Snodgrass/ McGraw production, the central figure is W. D., a poet of many guises, who encounters fire, darkness, brutish dissonances, but

does not succumb. In the end, in a final wordless scene—
McGraw's gouache titled "W. D.'s Midnight Carnival Friends"—
the poet mingles with the masquers, his guests at court, and
restores through his own luminous presence, the universal harmony. If, however, for the seventeenth-century audience the
meaning of the final revelry was fixed and clear, for McGraw and
Snodgrass it is the culmination of many perspectives carefully
layered throughout. Perhaps W. D. is a redemptive force or a silly
man, a gang leader or a universal victim. Metaphysics, contemporary events, myth, parody collide in this revelry. Here, its final
meaning is invented by each observer whose relationship to the
characters and events has been shaped by a number of points
of view.

In *The Death of Cock Robin*[10] McGraw and Snodgrass continue
to expand our way of seeing and to bring their use of the "curious
perspective" to its fullest development yet. The thirty-three
paintings and thirty-three poems are based on the eighteenth-
century nursery rhyme about the mysterious death of a bird
and the responses of beetle, owl, thrush, bull and others in the
ensuing rituals of acceptance and denial. McGraw reinvents the
nursery rhyme, Snodgrass reframes the narrative, and, together,
they transform a simple threnody for a child's mind into a witty
allegory for the modern mind. That mind, as the first gouache
and poem suggest, is an ingrown thicket where flowers conceal
thorns.

As in *The Fuehrer Bunker* and *Midnight Carnival,* when humor and seriousness meet in Snodgrass's mind, his wit is at its
most ingenious. In *Cock Robin* Snodgrass, for his part, concentrates on the opposition between Cock Robin and Mr. Evil. These
two incompatible figures serve Snodgrass's basic aesthetic that
"any very satisfying work of art is built upon a structure of op-
posing forces and attitudes, and that the more truly opposed
they are, the greater the work may become." Thus, as the narrative
unfolds, Cock Robin and Mr. Evil represent, at various points,
conflicts between good-evil, song-silence, imagination-reason,
love-hate, individuality-conformity, id-ego, nonstandard usage-
linguistic purity, schizophrenia-perfect sanity, and so on. The
and-so-on is important. There is no end to the conflicts and the
different forms they take.

But if indigenous conflict is the starting point, its complication is Snodgrass's primary concern. In fact, in *The Death of Cock Robin*, we do not even know If Cock Robin is dead. We are obliged to see the action through many spectacles—Mr. Evil's double-crossed eyes, Kafka's and Dostoevsky's contentious eyes, Words-worth's parodied eyes, the small eye of an ant, a mole's blind eye. We do not have linear perspective or a centric position. We have action which, to use a Snodgrass phrase, is "elusive, divergent, manifold." One voice tells us, "Somebody shot my bird down, somebody done him dirt." Another says,

> Who saw him die?
> Not I, certainly, says the fly;
> My dear, this polyhedral eye
> Can only make things out nearby.
> I mind my own bee's wax; that's my
> Alibi.

Who, then, are we to believe when, in various guises, Mr. Evil says that Cock Robin is dead, the fly can't be certain, the sparrow denies he did it if it was done, and W. D., who wants to keep Cock Robin alive, invents him so.

If action is inconclusive, so are the time and space which frame it. From the opening poem we find ourselves in internal and external worlds, and in fables, myths, and legends. In one poem alone, the historical moment gathers together Cock Robin, Robin Hood, Dr. Goebbels, Greek poetics, Nixon's "eighteen-minute gap," Bartók, and the Everly Brothers. Snodgrass's figures tend to be polymorphs living in "some funhouse, barbershop, Versailles / Hall of Mirrors." He begins several poems with such phrases as "The Brutish are Coming, the Brutish," and "Swing past, Miss Treavle, swing right by," and "My hat leaps up when I behold / A rhino in the sky." This allusive method, which superimposes worlds, is similar to the one that Snodgrass and McGraw used in their privately printed *To Shape a Song*,"[11] published in 1988. One poem begins "Open your eyes, now, W. D., / This is your life. If such there be." Another: "Out of the eggshell, fearlessly rocketting." Through an old TV program and a parody of a Whit-man poem, we immediately enter metamorphic worlds which become visually and thematically more complex as other per-spectives are embodied. On the TV screen, for example, W. D.

watching his life unfold before him (on a puppet show) is simultaneously a baby boy, young prince, Adam in the Garden, dunce in the corner, robin vs. worm, and a god vs. gods:

> You are yourself who stands aside
> To watch and witness, petrified.
> While vast universal powers collide
> In archetypal conflict to decide
> Whether good fortune or ill betide.
> Whether the robin with green face
> Would clench its claws in the wriggling, base
> Adder then soar, all craft and grace,
> Over your checkerboard of days
> Or should the serpent, sleek and wily,
> Slink through its goal where it might slyly
> Envenom the growing young boy vilely,
> Who sits like a stone grown soft with moss
> Seeming to take no thought of loss
> And making no move toward victory.
> This is your life if such there be.

The allusions are synchronistic, and this reality is more than the sum of its parts.

The young W. D. in *To Shape a Song* is the mature W. D. in *Cock Robin*, a figure who embodies the universal conflicts and whose life is a unique variation of an archetypal pattern. An archetype himself, W. D., indistinguishable at times from Cock Robin (a singer, independent, noisy, protective, imaginative, earthy, insecure, assertive) is not without his own subterfuges on his friend's behalf. As crafty as his adversary Mr. Evil, and as full of disguises, W. D. is also aware that his own mind is "a rank, unweeded / Veritable Africa where you / run guns or seek / unfathomable riches." W. D. contains both Cock Robin and Mr. Evil in himself. He is trapped in these polarities (as are many Snodgrass figures), but like the father/lover in *Heart's Needle* and *After Experience* and the son in *Remains*, he knows that "We try to choose our life" and that "We have to try" to love. The young W. D. is petrified into helplessness. "The whiner" in an earlier polyvoiced poem about self-preservation ("After Experience Taught Me . . ." in *After Experience*) is caught between a Spinoza-like speaker who would outlive death and a drill sergeant who would kill to avoid it. Unable to accept either proposition, "the whiner" is rendered inert by the magnitude of the problem:

> And you, whiner, who wastes your time
> Dawdling over the remorseless earth,
> What evil, what unspeakable crime
> Have you made your life worth?

But in *Cock Robin*, as we are led, not distracted, by the comic elements into our deepest exploration of Snodgrass's continuing concern with the self, W. D. accepts the challenge and commits the crime.

The "crime" W. D. commits is the negation of the single perspective—whether it be called Absolute, Ideal, or Truth. W. D. finds the world full of such perspectives: those who urge him to conform, "Be a horse of one congruous feather"; those who urge him to accept one of numerous "isms"—the "Merkans," for example, who "turn your equipment to mercantile uses" or the "Krishans" who "offer you visions / Of undying blisses / With premises, promises, / And crucifixes"; those who want "real ideals, / True cheerful thoughts—none of your idle / Moonin' about and moanin'." W. D. is interrogated, tempted, ostracized, and threatened by those who would make the self a product of a paradigm. His own songs, on the other hand, are often sour, "a cleverly, infernal / Dissonance"; he pumps with the "pulse that swells/ Lips, nails, all feverish parts"; with Cock Robin he has periods when his "whole nature splits in confusion / Of theories, beliefs, moods, and the profusion / Of goods and evils seems one vast delusion." From a world which would deny his drive to shape his own personality from his own experience, W. D. must flee. Thus, in "Disguised as Cock Robin, W. D. Escapes," he says,

> Come, Rosie Angel, faced with blues,
>   Join hands and we'll be piped together
>   Pilots of our own quarter, decked
> In multiplicity's fast hues—
>   This Joseph's cloak that many a feather
>   Weaves—in fact, a factory reject
>
> That is becoming without seems.
>   Fortuna's game wheel be our helm;
>   We'll shoot the jazzy straights of I-Am.

> Flee all Utopia's bonded schemes
> Of ideal bondage for a live realm. . . .

W. D.'s escape into "life" precludes resolution of conflicts and the achievement of any "comforting certainty." Snodgrass does not replace others' "bonded schemes" with his own. While universal powers collide around and within him, W. D. does not offer solutions, only perspectives—from the "back of an old kitchen chair," from both sides of Cock Robin's Magical Barricade, from "clouds of unknowing," from a "balance wheel of counterstrokes," from deep inside the mind. W.D.'s "wheel," with its "A stop foot, then a go foot . . . A fast foot, then a slow foot," is rational and balanced, it approximates Snodgrass's view of *irony* in modern criticism, a perspective which he admires—to a certain extent. But *constant* balance fosters stasis and that, Snodgrass says, promotes "a realm where things do not move (and so, perish)." It is another limiting, restrictive vision. So is its opposite—the escape into the "unconscious." For Snodgrass, imbalance must also be preserved—we find W.D. hidden deep in crimson "in forbidden / Urges, rage, lust, pride / Sweet murderous desires." He pushes the limits of seeing and experience, and Snodgrass is on record as saying that Art and the artist must always test limits to the utmost. But in a discussion of the complexities of love, he adds, who would want only "a world of open rage, of unlimited passion?". An unbalanced, a dadaist view, though insightful, is also limiting.

W. D. saves himself, and Cock Robin, by developing a wit which absorbs and creates angles of vision, expanding both his view of the world and his own self-perception. When Mr. Evil wants to determine the facts and establish that Cock Robin is dead, W. D. offers that the bird is alive in his mind, or wearing a disguise, or simply missing, or is rising naturally from the dead in

> some grander
> Land that schizophrenics
> Colonize from earth,
> One with the salamander,
> With the flaming Phoenix
> Or lodgepole pine whose clenched cones need
> The forest fire to cast their seed.

When Mr. Evil, who maintains a fixed view of the world and himself, assumes that he has the truth about all things, W. D. subjects him to a disconcerting demonstration of his own limits. He uses an *anagram* to redefine his adversary. Acknowledged by William Camden in his Renaissance study *Remains Concerning Britain* (Snodgrass's poetic study of his family is titled *Remains*) as a gem in the "*Alchimy of Wit*,"[12] this device is cleverly paradoxical. Applied by W. D. (in "W. D. Creates a Device for Inverting Mr. Evil"), it is subversive:

> Now, though you mouth me all things EVIL,
> I hear them through this medieval
> Antenna that receives what's VILE
> But transubstantiates its style,
> Sifting it through this sieve or VEIL
> Till all your meanest meanings fail
> And your commandments merely give
> Me one imperative verb: LIVE.

Against a narrow, blindered view, W. D., taking the same facts, transmutes evil into life, so that both live. "All things" are not evil, nor are they good. Both, in continuing contention, produce sudden revelations and reversals. Mr. Evil's words "get slam-dunked, codified, / Scrambled and then transmogrified." The result is an illumination—another way of seeing interrelationships, a new world, in fact, with a new meaning.

In Snodgrass's universe the diversity of perspectives is a reflection of the diversity of life, and the more angles one develops the more life one experiences. Consequently, Snodgrass seizes on forms of perception from any period. For example, Joseph Addison, the eighteenth-century arbiter of wit and critic of the Renaissance, in *The Spectator* papers (58–63), excluded from proper practice various poetic forms. Anagrams, acrostics, puns, shaped verse, and witches prayer were among examples of False Wit that were produced, said Addison, by "some of the most arrant undisputed Blockheads about the Town."[13] What Addison rejects Snodgrass gathers. In "Cock Robin's Roost Protects W. D. From Mr. Evil" COCK ROBIN'S MAGICAL BARRICADE acrostically defends W. D. from Mr. Evil and ends with a multiple pun that deepens the personal and mythical implications of the debate:

> Blinds men to their own faults. We
> Also share drives, all men being brothers;
> Relinquish this proud enmity.
>
> Our blood alliance shall B **R**
> True shame, a defect in the **I**
> Your double-cross-eyed poli-**C**
> Would dwindle and waste D 0 **A.**
>
> Drop such defences; we'll double you, De.
> Only across Styx, Mr. **E.**

In "W. D. Assists in Supporting Cock Robin's Roost" the shaped verse structure presents W.D., the earth, and their multiple stories as primary preservers of Cock Robin:

> . . . surely, no
> one would ever notice, maybe,
> that this 8-story bird house
> stands, or 8-bird story house
> was
> founded
> on a small
> round
> •

In "W. D. and Cock Robin Discuss the Dreaded Interrogation" the use of the witches prayer, an epigram which, says Addison, "fell into Verse when it was read either backward or forward, excepting only, that it Cursed one way and Blessed the other," provides a psychological clue. W. D. preparing to defend himself speaks nonsense: "Things such done never I've but; / Bring they can then charges what?" and "Hung get I, what matter no; / Tongue my disengage why so?" Read backward, however, his deepest fears make sense. Snodgrass constantly exposes the action to new angles of vision. We see the content and meaning expand as we view the basic conflict through many other forms: a police report, auction, anthem, catechism, lullaby, interrogation; through tercets, quatrains, quintets, sestets—in fact, in the poem "Credo," we stair-step from a couplet through twelve forms. In

the end, the accumulation of individual forms produces the overall effect that this whole universe is not fixed, defined, but still
evolving and still open to the imaginations which give it its
forms.

I do not think that Snodgrass's development of the curious
perspective and the metaphysical and baroque spirit of mind is
a retreat or detachment from the modern world. It may be his
response to T. S. Eliot's assertion that *Wit* though "precious and
needed" is "apparently extinct" in modern poetry[14]—his aesthetic response to an aesthetic challenge. But I think it has more
to do with Snodgrass's attempt to break through the limits which
the world and we ourselves impose upon our existence. That is
both an aesthetic and moral challenge. What *is* in the world, and
how many ways can we see it in order to know what we can get
away with? What *is* possible in the world?

Throughout both *W. D.'s Midnight Carnival* and *The Death of
Cock Robin* we hear many voices. At times we hear the unconscious where "lithe / goldfish swimming in a bowl, / slip through
the boughs and branches / as though veins and arteries / could
be the messengers of. . . . but / where did i begin?" At times we
hear the voices of the fancy:

> My socks slide off at the sight
> Of giant squids on high
> Or baby scorpions bubbling up
> Inside my morning coffee cup. . . .

At times nature speaks, authority speaks, novelists and singers
have words for us, the past petitions for our attention, the present
mingles with it. We hear foreign languages. Many voices speak
to us at once. The "Tattooed Man" in *Midnight Carnival* telescopes this process:

> how come i get no say what
>   my skin says, chances to write
> over, scratch out, explain explain *one*
>   *prize lamb. seven goats to be paid off*
> say like if your computer screen or
>   the Times Building ran fake newsreels,
> blue cartoons, **lasciate ogni Speranza**
>   accursed by my own gift of tongues

> with only future tenses i can't
> understand *shall forever be*
> *just as it has been* i am all bass
> ackwards in the mirror MEAN
> RAINFALL FOR 736 WILL RISE no man
> need testify against himself. . . .

Discord is Snodgrass's starting point, always. In his recent work—in this period of recording our dance in endless space—he has found the music/speech experiments in contemporary classical music compatible. In particular, Snodgrass's comment on Luciano Berio's *Sinfonia* is directly applicable to his own work. What fascinates Snodgrass about Berio's piece is that while the orchestra plays a Mahler scherzo, the Swingle Singers "speak in several languages, on divergent subjects, at various tempos, in many moods. The overall effect is enormously powerful: The result is not chaos but rather a very striking comment on the multiplicity, density, variousness of our world—on the way we must take meaning not from the sense of any one local phrase but from the overall movement of the whole."[15] Snodgrass's poems are voices in his own scherzo; as part of the collaboration with DeLoss McGraw their meaning expands. The world works that way, Snodgrass says, if we have our wits about us, if we experience it with an inventive mind.

Notes

1. W. D. Snodgrass, *In Radical Pursuit* (New York: Harper, 1975).

2. W. D. Snodgrass, "Giving Up Music," *Syracuse Scholar* 5 (Spring 1984): 78.

3. Arnold Stein, "On Elizabethan Wit," *Studies in English Literature 1500–1900* 1, 1 (Winter 1961): 80–81.

4. Philip Raisor, "Framing Portraits: An Interview with W. D. Snodgrass," *The Southern Review* 26,1 (1990): 70.

5. Jean H. Hagstrum, *The Sister Arts: The Tradition of Literary Pictorialism and English Poetry from Dryden to Gray* (Chicago: University of Chicago Press, 1958), xix.

6. Ernest B. Gilman, *The Curious Perspective: Literary and Pictorial Wit in the Seventeeenth Century* (New Haven and London: Yale University Press, 1978), 233.

7. W. D. Snodgrass and DeLoss McGraw, *W. D.'s Midnight Carnival*, (Encinitis: ARTRA, 1988).

8. Ben Jonson, "To Lady Mary Wroth," *Ben Jonson*, eds. C. H. Herford and Percy and Evelyn Simpson, 8 (Oxford: Oxford University Press, 1911), 1–6.

9. Robert M. Adams, ed., *Ben Jonson's Plays and Masques* (New York: Norton: 1979), 315.

10. W. D. Snodgrass and DeLoss McGraw, *The Death of Cock Robin* (Newark, London and Toronto: University of Delaware Press, 1989).

11. W. D. Snodgrass (with images by DeLoss McGraw), *To Shape a Song* (New York: Nadja Press, 1988).

12. William Camden, *Remains Concerning Britain,* ed. R. D. Dunn (Toronto: University of Toronto Press, 1984), 142.

13. Joseph Addison, *The Spectator,* ed. Donald F. Bond, vol. 1 (Oxford: Clarendon Press, 1965), no. 58, 245.

14. T. S. Eliot, "Andrew Marvell," *Selected Essays* (London: Faber, 1951), 304.

15. "Giving Up Music," 78.

W. D. Snodgrass's Poetic Music: The Artist as Orchestrator, Librettist, and Performer

ZACK BOWEN

WHEN I WAS IN FIFTH GRADE, DURING WORLD WAR II, OUR SCHOOL HAD newspaper collections every Friday. The three biggest boys in the school were set to work after lunch bundling the papers, a job we could do in an hour and a half, but since we were in no hurry to return to class, we spent three hours at the task. With time on our hands, one of my comrades in the war effort used to sit down in the basement gymnasium beating out the rhythms of various popular songs of the day ("Deep in the Heart of Texas," "Let's Remember Pearl Harbor," etc.) on an inverted metal trash barrel, and as we bundled we would try to guess from his rhythm what the song was. The point was not so much the talent of my percussionist colleague, but that the rhythm alone suggested to us the words, and thus the song.

We usually think of popular songs as music with words, but ignore the most obvious connection between the music and the lyrics: the all-important rhythm that binds the other two together. Back at the gym, more often than not we could figure out simply from the rhythmic thumping what the song was, especially since we had a very limited catalogue of musical selections from which to choose.

Years later, when W. D. Snodgrass came to a rehearsal for the University of Delaware English Department Annual Songfest, he suggested that we set various poems to incongruous musical settings, such as any of Emily Dickinson's poetry to "The Yellow Rose of Texas," or "The Rime of the Ancient Mariner" to the tune of "MacNamara's Band," or "Stopping by the Woods on a Snowy Evening" to "O Tannenbaum" or "The William Tell Overture." The audacity of the idea that such somber and serious poetry should consist of rhythmic patterns identical with those

61

of incongruously spritely tunes is the product of the mind of a
musician who is also a poet additionally gifted with a recognition of comic incongruity.

Incongruity, irony, and paradox are the stuff of all poets, but
the comic overlay is quite another thing. I don't mean to imply
by this comment that Snodgrass is an exclusively comic poet.
One has only to begin with *Heart's Needle* and later *The Fuehrer
Bunker* poems to realize the serious, even tragic, quality of much
of his finest work. But as Snodgrass himself tells us, even when
his poetry is about the last days of the Nazi hierarchy, the poems
deal with his characters as people, not as fascist or Elizabethan
icons, in much the same manner as his early confessional poetry
deals in realistic and truthful terms with his own universalized
emotions. What characterizes the work is its immediacy to our
present situation, the little details, foibles, petulance, and attitudes that give an aura of truth which infuses all Snodgrass's
poetry, no matter how divergent its subject matter.

However, this paper intends principally to address the influence of music on Snodgrass's language and technique. The latter
is often a technique which offers incongruity as a basic reality
of life. Perhaps the comic permanence of the incongruous is
what attracted him to early music. Snodgrass's *Six Troubadour
Songs* offers an interesting introduction for an investigation of
the effects of music on his poetry. In his preface to this brief
volume, Snodgrass talks about the difficulty of musicologists in
arriving at what those early songs actually sounded like:

> The source of the problem is that the notation in the manuscripts
> tells us the exact notes, but nothing of the rhythm. Following quite
> ingenious theories, but ignoring the Provencal verses, many musi-
> cologists have made thoroughly unsingable transcriptions—the mu-
> sical accents and the language stresses are locked in conflict. For the
> songs given here, I have made my own transcriptions; in each case
> my work is at variance with most musicologists . . . My only claim
> is that you can sing the Provencal words (and so my matching En-
> glish ones) to these renderings of the tunes.[1]

Paramount in Snodgrass's mind is that his song/poems must, like
their predecessors, first be singable, rather than artifacts on a

page. The songs are the vehicles of performance as much as they are segments of literature.

Snodgrass goes on to say that since the songs of Guillaume did not have recorded melodies, he merely went through the extant 276 melodies from the troubadour songs until he found one with the same verse form as the song he was translating. The game he was playing was not unlike our newspaper bundling sport: fitting the appropriate rhythm to a given set of words and hence the tune. The tunes themselves, are, as Snodgrass promised, singable in both the original and the English translation. A significant number were in minor keys, which provide the influence of Arabic or Andalusian music of North Africa to which he refers in the beginning of his introduction. Normally Western Europeans think of the minor key as associated with laments and doleful music, but, of course, that is not true of Middle Eastern music, which expresses all the emotions in minor keys. Still, the Troubadour songs are mixed with major and relative minor keys competing in different lines. The lines themselves are spiced with similar mixtures of sentiment, unsentimental lust, and longing, expressed in slightly incongruous, but accurate modern phraseology, such as "Some ladies get the rules all wrong," or "Let's take a nice warm bath, unwind, / Then take things slow."

At times Snodgrass will tease the readers into expectation that some contemporary phrase will win the comic day. In "The Peasant Lassy" the central line of each seven-line stanza is an iambic tetrameter ending in the feminine lassy. The song begins,

> Near a hedgerow, sometime recent
> There I met a shepherd lassy
> Full of mother wit and sassy,
> Some good peasant woman's lassy."

We wait for the entire poem—during which the articulate lassy gets the best of her would-be seducer—for the inevitable lassy/sassy rhyme once more, but it doesn't come until the coda:

> "Lass, I never met a lassy
> With a face so fair and sassy
> And a heart so cold and cruel,"
> "Sir, the owl gives you this saying:
> By an image, one man's praying
> While one gawks there like a fool."

The troubadour/persona has been vainly expecting her to succumb to his flattering expressions of her beauty and hints of
material gain, while the reader has been gawking at the poem in
expectation of the multisyllabic rhyme. In a way they have both
been rewarded intellectually if not passionately.

A similar situation occurs in the best music, when one harmonic ending is anticipated in the form of a normal chord progression, such as the one from dominant seventh to final tonic,
but instead something different occurs. A good example is the
series of chords at the end of the Rachmaninoff's "Prelude" in
C♯ minor, op. 3, no. 2. The five penultimate chords are anticipated
by a sustained C♯ octave in the base. Each of the chords, unex-
pected and perfect, each a small but magnificent variation on the
previous one, comes quietly, one after another, never completely
resolving the melodic line until a final thrice-repeated C♯ minor
chord ends the piece. Though Snodgrass's music is lighter, the
technique is the same, with one small variation: Snodgrass's six-
line coda shortens the song's seven-line stanza pattern, affording
both verbal contestants equal time, and concluding with an
accented syllable rhyme. The lassy has the last say, a sort of
recapitulation of her verbal victory, in just the same way Rachmaninoff repeated two inversions of the tonic C♯ minor triad at
the end of his "Prelude." There is an unmistakable finality about
each. Snodgrass, by his own admission, is a musician who never
gave up music, but transferred its impetus and passion to his
poetry. He talks about his early days at Iowa:

> I could indeed produce the qualities we then sought: intellectual
> compression, a brilliant texture, a surcharged rhythm and rhetoric.
> What was lacking? Only what [Swiss singer Hugues] Cuenod had in
> abundance: emotional (not intellectual) intensity; passion and a clear
> delineation of that passion's developing shape and impulse.[2]

So Snodgrass took his passion, structure, and formulation from
music, and his intense orality from musical performance. To a
singer, all human activity, especially the reading of poetry, is a
variety of performance. Music, unlike the plastic arts, is not a
static form. It exists in time as a series of auditory impulses,
rather than in space as sculpture or on a surface such as the
printed page or the canvas of a painting, and unless the audience

members are themselves musicians who can perform from notation, music requires an intermediary, an interpreter. Each interpretation varies, places the work into a new light, no matter how
subtle the changes appear to be. Often, especially in the late
nineteenth and early twentieth centuries, oratorios were dramatically altered, with grace notes added to melodic lines which
dramatically changed, or, as their practitioners would have
avowed, enhanced the musical intent. Poetry in the hands of an
oral artist like Snodgrass, carries a far greater performance value.
The passion Snodgrass refers to comes from the spontaneity of
performance; its reading (even at home in the reclining chair)
taking on the quality of interaction in much the same way a
musician or a singer interacts with musical notation, hearing or
singing it as he/she reads, and thus turning it into a public rather
than a private act. Such a response emphasizes its emotional
and musical qualities.

Music was early recognized by Karl Seashore and others to
possess attributes that could soothe maniacs in asylums and enhance output in the workplace, all the time playing on sublimi-
nal response and generating various emotions, including
passion. This emotional message is translated within exception-
ally intricate but rigid parameters of tone, harmonics, and time
(rhythm), like scientists' experiments under controlled labora-
tory conditions. Music can be written down and precisely timed,
with detailed instructions as to the specifics of its performance.
However, the wells of human response that varying individual
performances tap defy measurement. When Snodgrass refers to
"a clear delineation of that passion's developing shape and im-
pulse," he is talking about a form of poetry within rigorous
guidelines analogous to those of music, an artistic set of parameters in which to work and control and channel the passionate
intensity to artistic ends. In other words, the poet must be a
performer as well as a writer. At the very least he must orches-
trate his musically generated passion in such a way as to influence, if not place limitations on, his audience's response.

Snodgrass, besides being a superb performer on a variety of
ancient and modern stringed and percussion instruments, is a
gifted and trained singer. During the time we worked together
he was always buying precious guitars, especially instruments

made in a Mexican town which specialized in such instruments. The guitar provided the means of both singing and playing his music and poetry. It was performance art which dictated that its interpreter become identified personally with the subject matter of the song in order to accommodate the requisite feelings, and to publicize rather than internalize the product.

It was only natural, then, that Snodgrass, perhaps more than any other poet, revolutionized poetry readings. Back in the fifties, when I first began to attend performances of poetry, the fashion of the poet-readers was to drain their renditions of any emotion it possessed by reading in dull monotones, as if the poems were hieroglyphs properly carved on cave walls, rather than vital extensions of the oral tradition. Dylan Thomas's recorded readings did much to energize poetry reading, but his trained actor's voice was rivaled by Snodgrass's head resonance, and precise— even over-pronunciation—of nasals, final participles, and glottal stops. Singers who were trained in the fifties especially, still followed the school of projection which exaggerated common speech sounds, especially at the beginnings and ending of words, an exaggeration that in a concert hall enabled everyone on the last row to hear every word clearly, but sometimes lead to near burlesque affectations of speech. The trick became to enhance pronunciation to the point of near affectation but remain within the limits of standard pronunciation. Nasals and final affricates were voiced and resonance intensified, communicating every vocal segment with equal importance. One is aware of Snodgrass's immaculate pronunciation even in everyday conversation. It would take a circulatory stroke to curb the accuracy of his speech. Such extraordinary delivery makes the rhythms of his speech even more sensitive; the pitch, tone, intensity, and accents becoming more refined, even as they are subtly manipulated.

In a 1984 essay Snodgrass discussed the buried accent pattern of "Owls":

> I have . . . a poem about some great horned owls in which every line
> is a variation on the owl's call. The call consists of five notes:
>   HOO hoo-HOO, HOO, HOO.
> My poem begins:
>   Wait, the great horned owls . . .
> and every line proceeds to work variations on that rhythm.[3]

What Snodgrass neglected to mention is that it is practically impossible to utter the call accurately without dropping the pitch of the second, lowercase, hoo, and that the accented HOOs are not only separated by full stops, but remain on the same pitch. Rhythms form intricate complications with pitch in animals as well as human speech. Try reading any of the variations on the opening line of the first stanza without dropping the pitch of your voice at the unaccented syllables:

> Wait: the great horned owls
> Calling from the wood's edge; listen.
> There: the dark male, low
> And booming, tremoring the whole valley.
> There: the female, resolving, answering
> High and clear, restoring silence.
> The chilly woods draw in
> Their breath, slow, waiting, and now both
> Sound out together, close to harmony.[4]

Reciting the four foot lines without any drop in pitch results in merely mechanical machinelike reproduction. The minor variations on the metric pattern are all in relatively low-pitched, unaccented syllables, a spoken cadence shared by both music and speech, but in the case of "Owls" one in which a singer/poet has paid special attention to concluding syllables, the products of feminine ending variations.

Snodgrass further admits in his article that the cadences of at least some of his poems come from music: "In another recent poem, a belly dancer appears. That poem works variations on an old American show tune, 'Heat Wave': 'We're having a heat wave; a tropical heat wave.' My poem starts: 'Like battered old mill-hands, they stand in the orchard' and proceeds to work variations on that rhythm."[5] Singers especially have a tendency to do what my newspaper-bundling buddy did: hear the music as rhythmic cadences. As a singer myself, I am constantly applying names and phrases I hear to incongruous melodies, especially to songs whose words seem grotesquely sentimental, such as "Dream the Impossible Dream." One needs only a minimally creative scatological mind to apply to the three-stress line with a penultimate four syllable word, any of the degrading parodies that have occurred to me over the years, none of which have any place on these scholarly pages. The point is that, like Snodgrass—and even lacking his poetic genius—my experience as a singer is so much a part of my subconscious as to erupt suddenly and without warning when the right cadences trigger them.

If Snodgrass's language is influenced by music, so too is his structure. In *The Fuehrer Bunker*, Snodgrass informs us,

> oppositions and incongruities work constantly as a principle of composition. First, there are the voices of different characters—figures from Hitler's government or his private life—with the disparate vocal qualities of their various personalities, techniques and aims. Each, moreover, has his or her characterizing verse form. For some characters this is further complicated by the inclusion of musical quotations, usually arising from some darker, less recognized area of the mind. . . .
>
> The simplest verse forms here are wide-open free verse pieces built on a simple straightforward antiphony. . . . Hitler's mistress, Eva Braun, has poems which balance her conscious thoughts against those melodies she finds herself singing from time to time and which suggest something of her unconscious thoughts—"Tea for Two" or parts of the Catholic wedding mass.[6]

The disparate voices of the characters sing against each other, in different cadences and verse forms, like the conflicting melodic lines in Wagnerian opera or twentieth-century classical music. Together they form a chorus at once discordant, various, banal, and lyrical, a single multiperspective on the inner tumult of off-base people who commit crimes which defy human compassion or logic, but who are strangely ordinary themselves. One might well ask if such a mixture of antisocial behavior, cruelty, and banality is representative of the human race as a whole. Eva's references to "Tea for Two" recall Joyce's Gerty MacDowell with her innocent fascination with popular culture. The patterns of thematic and psychological association emanating from the song lines interspersed in the marginalia of Eva's first poem, and the passages from the wedding mass in her second both emulate Joyce's use of music to trigger stream of consciousness associations in Sirens. Joyce, who also was a singer and musician of professional or near professional status, may well have provided in *Ulysses* even more stylistic models for *The Fuehrer Bunker*. Like the later half of *Ulysses*, each *Fuehrer Bunker* episode is written in a different style. Goebbels's poem is interspersed with newspaper heads or subheads, as is Joyce's Aeolus episode, and the last head is the longest and most ironic, verging on the comic, the same pattern as Aeolus.

The Death of Cock Robin poems also share structural similarities with The Fuehrer Bunker cycle: the diversity of verse forms, the antiphonal quality of the poems as choral responses to each other, and above all the infusion of the singer or poet into the characters, adapting their personas almost as extensions of himself. The tactic had the effect of exposing the humanness of the Teutonic crowd in The Fuehrer Bunker, but is far more complex in Cock Robin. First of all, there are two performers or intermediaries between the poems and the audience: Snodgrass and De-Loss McGraw, the collaborating artist. Both assume the role normally occupied by the actor or singer. In addition Cock Robin is a songbird with a well-established song of his own, unjustly accused, suffering at the bar of injustice, and verbally excoriated by a Grand Inquisitor figure, that old liar, Mr. Evil. W. D. is himself a character sympathetic, analytical, solacing the songbird, but always realizing his affinity—even identification—with the bird. If one examines the titles of the poems, twenty-three designate W. D. as Protagonist; four, Cock Robin; five, neither; and in one they share the title. Taken as a whole, then, the suite is about an image of a songbird/poet-philosopher and his rational other, W.D. Both characters are in effect singers or performers of a metaphor for Snodgrass's attempt to redeem himself on a public stage for The Fuehrer Bunker, a work which was never a crime to begin with. Snodgrass, as interpreter or performer, mitigated his grim vision of life in The Fuehrer Bunker by making his characters into people rather than evil icons, and later, in Cock Robin, he metaphorized his difficulty with the critical reception of his earlier poems. He told Philip Raisor,

I was thinking, I confess, when I was writing the Cock Robin poems about the very bad reception I got from people for The Fuehrer Bunker. They didn't want to hear what I was singin" and while on the one side I would like to be received a little more warmly and generously, at the same time the fact that people reject the poems as violently as they often do and on such shaky terms leads me to think that, yeah, maybe I did just what I wanted to do. Maybe the poems

have a chance, maybe they're O. K. Maybe I was singin' better than
people want you to.[7]

Snodgrass thus provides his own defense in the Cock Robin
metaphor. "W.D." is a singer and interpreter, taking a nursery
rhyme and a lot of other musical forms and fitting a situation
analogous to his own to their protagonist/interpreter, and then
reinterpreting "W.D.'s" own interpretations in a Chinese Box not
unlike those created by John Barth. Yeats's question about telling
the dancer from the dance gains new meaning when we add the
collaboration of a painter with his own interpretation of everything, which informs and influences Snodgrass about "W.D." on
the bird, all ultimately one and the same. One is tempted to
wonder whether the artist, McGraw, is also a Snodgrass creation.

Snodgrass's new tone in the Cock Robin poems is playful, often
light and full of razzle-dazzle, multisyllabic rhymes and spec-
tacular verbal tricks and forms, but at the same time the world
it depicts is principally one of accusation, rancor, and death.
The humor is often of the gallows variety, to borrow a metaphor
from another prophetic suite of Snodgrass's poems, *Gallows
Songs*.

The Cock Robin series, based on a nursery rhyme remembered
by many as a song and by others as a poem, uses a range of
musical forms. Snodgrass utilized the most easily identifiable
musical pattern to supply the clearest message, in "W. D.'s
Blues":

> Somebody shot my bird down; somebody done him dirt:
> Somebody shot my bird down; somebody done him dirt;
> Hangs his head like someone scorned and feelin' hurt.

Despite Cock Robin's former popularity, and his subsequent fall
from grace, W. D. vows to keep one feather from Cock Robin
tucked in his hatband in case W. D. ever writes a song. The blues
lament ends on a note of defiant joy:

> Gonna fly Cock Robin's feather like a bright kite in the sky;
> Gonna fly Cock Robin's feather like a bright kite in the sky;
> Run it up my flagpole just to keep my spirits high.

Thus, Snodgrass is back where he began, a confessional poet singing songs of himself, his sadness, and his defiant joy. As his own interpreter, his own singer, he continues to occupy center stage in contemporary American poetry.

Notes

1. W. D. Snodgrass, *Six Troubadour Songs* (Providence: Burning Deck, 1977).
2. W.D. Snodgrass, "Giving Up Music," *Syracuse Scholar*, 5, 1 (Spring 1984): 70.
3. Ibid., 73.
4. W.D. Snodgrass, *Selected Poems 1957–1987* (New York: Soho, 1987), 183.
5. "Giving Up Music," 73.
6. Ibid., 74.
7. Philip Raisor, "Framing Portraits: An Interview with W.D. Snodgrass," *The Southern Review*, 26, 1 (Winter, 1990): 70–71.

The Music of "Each in His Season"

Fred Chappell

Upon first reading "Each in His Season," the sequence that gives W. D. Snodgrass's eighth volume of poetry its title, I surmised that it was very closely modeled after the familiar cycle of concertos by Antonio Vivaldi called *The Four Seasons*. This hypothesis turned out to be inexact, but the poet did indeed begin his work with ideas of musical organization and development in mind, and I stand assured that Vivaldi provided inspiration and suggestion though not a structural template.

Readers familiar with Snodgrass's work will hardly be surprised. The poet is an accomplished musician and an ardent amateur musicologist and has often taken music as subject matter for his poetry. A poem like the splenetic "A Curse" in *Each in His Season* reveals how intimately he is involved with music, while such poems as "Minuet in F♯," "Mexican Hat Dance," and "Tap Dance: W. D. Escapes from Miss Treavle" demonstrate his delight in fitting language tightly to well-known melodies. But these verses, for all their verbal and metrical ingenuity, are in the nature of exercises, jeux d'esprit, while "Each in His Season" is an ambitious and complex effort.

There is, moreover, a close connection between the poet and this composer. Most people hear Vivaldi's cycle by means of radio play or Muzak speakers in medical offices or supermarkets and the majority are unaware that each of the concertos is prefaced by a poem whose lines the music illustrates in methodical programmatic fashion. These prefatory sonnets are generally attributed to the composer himself, for it is obvious that whoever wrote the music had a perfect knowledge of the poetry.

Here is the first sonnet in Vivaldi's sequence:

> *Primavera*
> Giunt' e la Primavera e festosetti
>   La salutan gl' Augei con lieto canto,
> E i fonti allo spirar de Zeffiretti
>   Con dolce mormorio scorrono intanto.

Vengon' coprendo l'aer di nero amanto
E Lampi, e tuoni ad annuntiarla eletti
Indi tacendo questi, gl' Augeletti,
    Tornan' di nuovo al lor canoro incanto:

E quindi sul fiorito ameno prato
    Al caro mormorio di fronde e piante
Dorme 'l Caprar col fido can' a lato.

    Di pastoral Zampogna al suon festante
Danzan Ninfe e Pastor nel tetto amato
    Di primavera all' apparir brillante.

Spring
The Springtime's come around again and merrily
    Small birds salute the season as they sing;
    Now zephyrs sigh across the waters airily
    Which answer back with their sweet murmuring.
Soon, though, the sky is cloaked in robes of black;
    Thunder and lightning come—Springtime's loud heralds.
    But once the storm subsides and calm comes back
    The birds, just as before, take up their carols.
Where the green meadow flowers all around,
    Amidst soft whisperings of leaves and plants
    The goatherd sleeps next to his faithful hound.
Now shepherds' bagpipes start the revelling;
    Under clear skies the nymphs and shepherds dance
    Decked out in the full radiance of the Spring.

This translation of the sonnet is Snodgrass's own and appears in the volume, *The Four Seasons*, published by Targ Editions of New York in 1984. It is a handsome book, containing not only the Italian sonnets with translations on facing pages, but also passages from the score that meticulously illustrate the substance of the words. There is also a short foreword by Snodgrass which explains why he undertook the project and its importance.

For a long time, *The Four Seasons* was performed without reference to the four sonnets that were not only printed as prefaces to the concertos in the earliest editions of the scores but were also "broken into lines and groups of lines and either printed directly above that part of the music which embodies its contents, or else represented there by capital letters referring back to the complete sonnet at the beginning." Snodgrass notes

that Vivaldi also places headings over the staves to indicate narrative elements and gives occasional directions to instrumental-
ists on how to make the musical notes more imitative of the
actions and objects of the poetry. The sonnets are important, he
argues, for without them, the musical interpretation is unfaithful.
"By willfully ignoring these—Vivaldi's express directions—most
performers have reduced this movement to sheer and, I think,
cloying prettiness, banishing that element of annoyance without
which the scene cannot embody its right balance of opposed
qualities."

The movement referred to is the slow second movement that
illustrates the third strophe of the sonnet: Where the green
meadow flowers all around,

> Where the green meadow flowers all around,
>   Amidst soft whisperings of leaves and plants
>   The goatherd sleeps next to his faithful hound.

In his biography, *Vivaldi: Voice of the Baroque* (Thames and
Hudson, 1993), H. C. Landon Robbins provides a very brief description of the concerto movement that represents these lines:

> The solo violin, in dreamy melody, represents the sleeping goat-herd.
> The two violins move in quiet dotted rhythms, telling us of the mead-
> ows rippling under a soft May wind. In an incredible stroke of ge-
> nius, the entire rest of the music is given to the violas . . . which
> describe 'il cane che grida,' the dog which many of us have heard
> howling or barking at the moon on a still moonlit night in a solitary
> northern Italian landscape. Vivaldi has even caught the dog's
> rhythm—woof-*woof,* woof-*woof,* woof-*woof.*

The biographer gives us to understand that this passage is ame-
nable to a great deal of further close analysis of its rhythms,
harmonies, figures, and sound effects as they accord with the
words of the poem. No nuance of the composer's sonnet is left
unremarked by his score.

These nuances Snodgrass has striven to reproduce in English:
"in translating these sonnets I have tried not only to approximate
the original's metre and rhyme scheme but, far more important,
its exact order of phrasing. Thus my lines, like their Italian counterparts, may be extracted and set at the proper places in the

score. They might also be read aloud as a part of the performance; I believe they should be. Certainly, the presence of the quotations from the poems either in the performance or in the score illuminates and enlivens one's grasp of the music."

A similar program, I would maintain, underlies "Each in His Season." The big difference is the obvious one: the poet cannot sound instrumental music from the pages of his volume and so must supply a comparable verbal music. His ambition to write an evocative verbal music was in fact the motive that inspired the sequence. Snodgrass's verse has always occupied itself with musical effects of various sorts but nowhere are they more precisely calculated or more thoroughly executed than in these four suites of poems. His translations of the Vivaldi sonnets show just how expert he is in such practice.

A line of poetry can sound only one tone at a time, word by word, and yet by means of full rhyme and slant rhyme, enjambment, compound words, couple-rhymes, and puns, Snodgrass can suggest to the cultivated ear triads, dissonances, key changes, close harmonies, tone clusters, and inversions. These effects can work by analogy only and it would surely be an error to make simple identifications, to say that a slant rhyme "equals" a musical dissonance or an anagram like "lips slip" ("Spring Suite, i") is the same thing as a harmonic inversion or that a compound like "punk-spiked" ("Spring Suite, viii") is identical to a tone cluster. The qualities of pitch, measure, and rhythm can never be so clearly defined in speech as they can be tonally. Yet once our attention is alerted to the poet's purposes, the mind and ear can begin to apprehend musical design.

Though we may not strictly identify such simple full rhymes as "shoots / roots," "found ground," "decay / our clay" with triads, I do think we can confidently describe them as consonances, as sounds which communicate the same ease and satisfaction that triadic harmonies afford. And if we cannot authoritatively assert that slant rhymes and near-rhymes stand for seconds or minor seconds, surely we can call them dissonances—especially in phrases like "The turtles / turntail on the pond" ("Autumn Variations, ii") where Snodgrass follows the first word immediately with its near-rhyme and emphasizes the relationship with enjambment over the line break. If Vivaldi may be allowed his dog barks and cuckoo calls, then Snodgrass should be allowed his onomatopoeic pleasures too, the songs of starling ("Spring Suite, viii") and lark ("Summer Sequence, i").

The four suites bear these titles, "Spring Suite," "Summer Sequence," "Autumn Variations," and "Snow Songs," and each is made up of eight to ten separate poems. The poems differ from each other formally, but each suite irregularly alternates verses in rhyme or sometimes rhymeless measure with poems in free verse. Each suite begins with an introductory poem and ends with a coda verse that restates, usually in fresh terms, the themes of the whole; in the first three sequences the final poems also offer transition, by means of thematic foreshadowing, to the following sequences. Each poem in the suites takes up a new theme or metaphor while still maintaining some relationship, by verbal recall or motivic implication, with many of the other poems.

In these ways too the works of Snodgrass and Vivaldi resemble one another. The concertos are broken in the traditional manner into three large movements, each with different formal characteristics and moods, yet all still related thematically and harmonically. The movements too are broken into sections, each taking up a new idea, treating it in unique fashion but subjecting it to the larger architectural requirements. In the final movement of "L'Inverno," for example, Vivaldi represents walking on thin ice by composing a violin solo that "slithers about in quavers with no supporting harmonies whatever," according to Landon Robbins. Then comes a section of slurred quavers, "walking very carefully so as not to slip." But then we do slip and fall to the ground ("cader a terra," says the sonnet), and the violin represents this action also. Then come sections in which the ice breaks, the south wind blows outside doors shut fast, and the north wind arrives to do battle with the other winds—and all these actions are imitated by, and are clearly identifiable in, the notes.

These are the effects that Snodgrass strives to reproduce, not only with verbal descriptions of certain actions and phenomena, but also by means of verse technique. The first of the "Snow Songs" tells of driving a car through a sudden snow squall. The snowflakes become a metaphor for all living species and their brief time of existence, their emergence from dark eternity and their return to it. Using caesurae and syntax, the poet renders not only the import but also the sensations of the circumstance:

one. now another. one
more. some again; then done.
though others run
down your windshield when
up ahead a sudden
swirl and squall comes on
like moths, mayflies in a swarm
against your lights, a storm
of small fry, seeds, unknown
species, populations—every one
particular and special; each one
melting, breaking, hurling on
into the blank black. soon
never to be seen again.
most never seen.
all, gone.

Here the poet contrives effects comparable to those parts of
the adagio of Vivaldi's "Summer" that illustrate his line, "E de
mosche, e mossoni il stuol furioso!" in which angry swarms of
gnats and flies surround the hapless shepherd. The composer
represents the agitated swarms with repeated dotted notes in
violins and cellos while the sullen whine of the insects sounds
from a languorous solo violin. Snodgrass employs repetitious
droning rhythm and slant rhyme—*when, sudden, unknown,
again, soon*—to reinforce his metaphor of the swarm-storm of
insect species, while the base rhyme-word *one* (occurring four
times) emphasizes the uniqueness of each individual life, "particular and special." This use of rhyme is a swiftly economical
way to show unity-in-multeity.

The rhythm too is ingenious and close to Vivaldi in spirit. The
first two lines contain five full stops, a figure for the hesitant
intermittent beginning of a snow squall. With the third line
words start to come thick and fast and the lines are tightly en-
jambed and the verse picks up even more speed with the catalogue that occupies lines 6–9. The sudden full stop in line 9
marks the turning point of the squall (the dash recalls the musical sign for a whole-note rest) and the rhythm begins to slow as
caesurae become more pronounced. The poem ends ritardando
and diminuendo with five full stops and the long nasal hum, *n*.

A careful reading will surely discover more of Snodgrass's musical usages in the first poem of "Snow Songs," but its purpose

as a thematic introduction must be remarked also. The theme is
the double one of individual death and the disappearance of
species. Winter and snow are traditionally symbolic of the end
of a human life and the dormancy of earth, but Snodgrass seems
to intend a final winter, a season that leads to no springtime, the
Fimbul Winter that follows Ragnarok.

The second poem in this sequence compares snow to the confetti of a ticker-tape parade, a confetti that obscures the world,
"a near-zero / visibility / where nothing can be / known sure of
events." The third poem continues the idea of snow as obliteration, as history disappears from memory as if daubed over by a
bookkeeper's correction ink. The fourth alludes to the same line
of thought, "Thick snow blots out the maps"; and the fifth uses
the image of whitewash for the same purpose. In the sixth poem
the great snowfall has covered all the world and human survivors
live within its depths like sea creatures at the bottom of an ocean.
The sardonic seventh poem ends with an explicit image of an
individual death when a snow-white coverlet is drawn over the
face of a dying patient. The final poem of the final sequence is
spoken by that figure familiar in Norse, Icelandic, and Anglo-
Saxon poetry, the Last Survivor; he is the poet and he sees himself as being out of place now in a deserted universe, his voice
on his page of written poetry growing as silent and incommuni-
cative as the visage of a corpse under a death mask.

These last lines are almost the only self-referential ones in the
whole work and they make an effective coda because they lead
us to think of the sequence as a whole, recalling all the previous
themes and techniques, the music and the matter of the poems
we have just read. This poem does not possess the direct tone of
that famous quotation from Job—"I only am escaped alone to
tell thee"—because Snodgrass has distanced the poet from his
work with a canny use of the second person pronoun; the use
of "I" would be grossly intrusive, out of key with the formal
tonality of the whole:

> Still the snow
> falls—as a clean sheet smooths
>   your shape out of the bed
>   you don't go back to.
>   You are the missing

                    tooth, the one place
          at the table, lost
                         wax from the casting—though,
               while they last,
          these chicken scratchings hold
                         the voice unspoken on
               the finished page as under
                              plaster hardening,
          a fading face.

A gloomy conclusion. But neither is Vivaldi in any jolly frame
of mind. His "Primavera," though interrupted by a storm, is
cheerful enough and ends with nymphs and shepherds footing
it in the chequer'd shade. But his "L'Estade" is rent by continual
tempest and concludes with a picture of crops destroyed by hail.
"L'Autunno" seems pleasant at first with its harvest festival and
peasant dance, but a hunting scene ends the poem with a scene
of the prey exhausted by the chase, confused by the clamor of
dogs and guns, scarred with wounds, and trembling in the lan-
guishment of death ("Già sbiogottita, e lassa al gran rumore / De
schioppi e canni ferita minaccia / Languida di fuggir, mà op-
pressa muore"). The last line of "L'Inverno" declares that being
snug indoors is the way to have joy in the wintertime, but the
preceding thirteen present only snowstorms, winds that bring
asthma, cold feet, chattering teeth, rain, and ice that causes acci-
dents. Franz Joseph Haydn used the long pastoral sequence *The
Seasons* by James Thomson as Ur-text for his celebrated oratorio,
but neither Antonio nor W. D. Snodgrass concur with Thomson's
sanguine conclusion:

          The storms of Wintry Time will quickly pass,
          And one unbounded Spring encircle all.

There is, however, one similarity between the British poet's
purposes and those of Snodgrass. Vivaldi is not content to paint
scenes of nature; he includes human activity in both his music
and his poetry. But he shows only emblematic action, limited
vignettes that characterize each season; his scene-painting is like
that we find on Seasons plates of majolica or Dutch blue-and-
white. Thomson's many pages of spacious blank verse allow him
room to spin fables as well as to depict nature, to include anec-

dotes and pursue speculations, and to indulge in general social and philosophical commentary.

The following lines, taken almost at random, offer a common example of the latter tendency; here Thomson expatiates upon the relationship between Poetry and Philosophy (personified as "thee"):

> Tutor'd by thee, hence poetry exalts
> Her voice to ages; and informs the page
> With music, image, sentiment, and thought,
> Never to die; the treasure of mankind,
> Their highest honour, and their truest joy!

Snodgrass follows this practice of including social and moral commentary in his nature writing, but he does not divagate in the manner of James Thomson. His comments do not take the form of asides but entertain various aspects of the controlling metaphor of each poem. In "Snow Songs, ii," for example, the central comparison is that snow is like the confetti showered upon a ticker-tape parade for "some departing hero." But the figure of this hero is soon obscured by the uncertainties of history and by those who destroy its annals. The confetti falls wilder and thicker until it blurs the scene:

> Now, into a near-zero
> visibility
> where nothing can be
> known sure of events,
> what with the pervasive, dense
> smother of shredded documents.

The irony is mordant but just: the departing hero is celebrated with confetti made of those same documents he shredded in order to hide his misdeeds. But in obscuring history by destroying evidence he also obscures the image of himself. The figures of President Nixon and Colonel Oliver North come inevitably to mind, and Snodgrass's speculation that we shall never really know who they were and are, because we shall never know what they have done, is probably true.

The form of "Snow Songs, ii" mirrors the events it describes: the thick texture of snowfall and parade confetti is displayed as rhymed couplets in iambic trimeter, "a dense smother" of versification that is relieved in the next poem by unrhymed free verse. Snodgrass often intersperses his elaborate and sometimes persnickety forms with looser lines; the contrast points up the virtues of both poetic idioms and offers some of the same tension/relaxation qualities that we find in the musical counterposing of allegro and adagio tempos and melodic lines.

Though the Snow Songs ii and iii contrast formally, the poet binds them thematically. The second song ends with the departing hero become nonvisible in the snowstorm of celebratory confetti; the third song opens with a similar image of corrective obliteration: "White out; white out; so / that the landscape's ledger / balances again." Shredded documents and the bookkeeper's correction fluid are instruments of revisionist history. Winter snow is like revisionist history in that it covers up the ceaseless impolite operations of nature, the decay of life and the recycling of matter; the remains of a dead white-tailed deer "are spirited / away like laundered funds." This latter phrase once more recalls Nixon and North, of course, but this third song goes on to an even more pessimistic thought. Not only does revisionist history cover up actual events, but true history disappears too, as a society tries and succeeds in forgetting the horrors it has witnessed. The snow obliterates the landscape in the way that western nations have erased from their memories the Russian sacrifices during the siege of Stalingrad:

> Stalingrad will be no more
>> than scattered fading photographs,
> just some aging soldiers'
>> recollections till at last
>>> all thought dies down to the
> perfection of a blank page
>> and the lighted
>>> screen that will flick off.

Thus, winter snow is established as a trope for the loss, sometimes purposeful, of historic truth over time. These are the main elements of the theme of "Snow Songs" and each of the eight separate poems is a variation on this theme that is sometimes disguised but never abandoned. In the fourth song, the birds that have migrated are compared to the absconders of public funds;

in the fifth, the omnipresent snow seems to be the product of our own vices as well as the product of nature—face powder, cocaine, fungus mold, bird dung, and whitewash, a term that once more reminds us of the cover-up of political malfeasance. The sixth poem returns to the metaphor of the first, snowflakes as individual members of dying species, but now the scene is like an underwater landscape and the species is not mayflies or moths but diatoms that expire and drift down to create the ocean floor, that is, the substratum of history. The seventh snow poem begins lightly enough as flakes are compared to "lace paper valentines" and "bitsy webs and doilies." Soon enough, though, these become peekaboo bras and scanties, styrofoam popcorn, and the other trivialities so thickly littering our landscape that it is transformed into a "dull white coverlet" to be drawn over the eyes of a hospital patient whose chances of survival are poor. The final poem, darkest of them all, accepts the death of humankind and the disappearance of its history as a condition that is fitting as well as inevitable; it is the anomaly of the poet's endeavor, his futile "chicken scratchings" upon the white page, that is distressing. Let him too no longer be "the one place at the table," the wax that is lost in a cire perdu casting. Let him too be part of the universal whiteness that, like Alexander Pope's Dulness, "buries all."

The principal characteristics of "Each in His Season" are, then, these: formal virtuosity and experimentation in the pursuit of musical qualities, description of natural process and landscape, *paysage moralisé*, elegiac lament, and social satire. This is hardly a usual colligation of purposes for a poem, even a poem in large sequences broken down into separate parts, and the problems and difficulties are easy to discern.

In the first place, there is the danger that many will overlook the musical analogy. It is not necessary that a reader know thoroughly Vivaldi's concerto cycle; *The Four Seasons* is an inspirational but not an architectural model for Snodgrass. But if one does not intuit at least a dim notion of musical analogy, some of the principles of composition and organization will go unapprehended. Not recognizing these, a reader is apt to find certain sections, and even the sequence as a whole, wildly eccentric, so odd in method and appearance as to be off-putting.

Well, "Each in His Season" *is* an eccentric performance. It is not nearly as outré as some pages of, say, Frank Bidart or Susan Howe, but it is likely to sound choppy if improperly read and to seem disjointed if the necessary connections are not grasped. But once one understands that the poetic forms are supposed to suggest musical forms and that the underlying principle of organization is also musical—*tema con variazione*—then this sequence of poems clarifies in intention and its methods of execution are open to examination and appreciation. In this way, "Each in His Season" resembles a great many other modernist works: its surface looks ragtag and arbitrary, but the apprehension of an organizing principle reveals firm structural design. A string quartet by Schoenberg offers the same perplexities and resolution, as do Cubist paintings by Braque and Picasso.

Even so, not all difficulties vanish with a wave of the baton. The well-disposed reader willing to allow the poet his musical analogies and assenting to his theme-and-variation organization may still find some passages slippery going. What may seem to the poet an acceptable, even an obvious, variation upon an announced theme may seem to his audience a puzzling leap to another topic entirely. Musical variations are controlled by given melodic and harmonic progressions; there is an unbreakable inner logic tying any valid variation to its original theme. Such exact means are not available to the poet who must sometimes make associations where the connections are obscure to his audience.

"Summer Sequence" offers an apt example. The dominant theme of these ten poems is satiety; the season is overfull, with a ripeness verging on the rotten. It is like a nation puffed up with its wealth—smug, bullying, worshipful of machines and of force, corrupt, and overly ambitious. Here, as in other sections, Snodgrass offers an allegorical vision of a certain period of American history; glancing topical references to a green "beret and uniform / of creeping vines," to Plato's Cave (here the notorious New York sex club), and to psychedelic spray paint, indicate which years he has in mind.

"Summer Sequence, ii" presents a vision highly similar to that of the conclusion of Vivaldi's "L'Estade." A storm wreaks dire destruction on the groves and fields:

> All night black tree
> shapes wrestled their dark
> angels or assailants; the deep woods
> wracked by shattering, cracking;
> then rain drove straight
> sheets like a wave's crash
> wrenching leaves and birds' nests
> from the branch, battering
> grain flat in the fields;
> mice, rabbits in their burrows
> drowned.

"L'Estade" ends with a like disaster: "Tuona e fulmina il Ciel e grandinoso / Tronca il capo alla spiche e a'grani alteri." The sky is all huge thunder and lightning that decapitates the wheat and the other crops.

Vivaldi stops there, but Snodgrass goes on to depict the ironically peaceful and deceptively cleansed aftermath:

> At first dawn, soft
> mists down the valley rise till
> light strikes, enamelling
> each emerald green leaf
> splattered clean.

This green is the dominating—or domineering—color of "Summer Sequence," but it is not a hue implying the innocence of youth. In the third poem it is compared to a forest fire and a virus. The fifth poem interprets the color as concupiscence, with a bitter parody of a famous line by Federico Garcia Lorca: "Green; we're greedy for you, green." In the ninth poem this fat summer greenery is money, impure and simple, and the effects of its corruption are more deadly and more durable than even the summer storms and the territorial combats of birds have been:

> Deregulated summer rolls on:
> Our meadow's making hay as if
>   the national gross product must be
> grass, the duty of all flesh: get high
>   as your eye by the Fourth of July.

> Fledged, open-eyed, the rough young
> bluejays squall like soccer fans

crammed in their twiggy stadium—loud
disciples of some new rock star, cure-all
    politics or new saviour: greed.

    Nothing will come of nothing: things
lead on to things: the ad campaign's still
    on though the summer's till brims over.
Sunflowers smile down like visitors
    to Plato's Cave or brazen bank examiners,

    where shameless, coarse young leaves spread
open to the sun. Through ditch and hedgerow
    kudzu carries out its hostile
takeover; the greenback reigns. Our
    scriptures: lovecharts, popcharts and the Dow.

This is the coda of "Summer Sequence" and in it Snodgrass
attempts to tie up the salient themes from all the poems preceding: money, fraud, lust, aggression, immodesty, hypocrisy, cultural and spiritual pollution. The metaphors and images include
these: libertine economic policies, bluejays at a soccer stadium
applauding a rock star, a pointless advertising campaign, sunflowers and bank examiners visiting a sex club, kudzu buying
out General Motors, sex manuals, the Top Forty, and the Dow
Jones averages. When Dr. Johnson complained of metaphysical
poetry that it yoked the most heterogeneous ideas by violence
together, he might have been describing "Summer Sequence, ix."

Snodgrass shall have recognized this wild disorder, of course,
and it surely is deliberate, a parody upon his own idea of approx-
imating a musical coda by means of spoken language. The lines
insist upon their incongruities and absurdities and the resulting
phantasmagoria comes out as a burlesque of the coda concept.
The effect produced is that of stretto, in which phrases of a fugue
subject tumble over one another so closely that the intensity is
raised to a high pitch. Sometimes self-mockery is intended, as
in the uproarious conclusion of Bartók's *Concerto for Orchestra*,
and I believe that a similar aim motivates Snodgrass in "Summer
Sequence, ix."

This crazy-quilt confusion of images and tropes and the heavy
moralizing make up one more instance of W. D. Snodgrass's bear-
ish humor. With its puns on *gross* and *grass*, on *duty*, on *still*
and *-'s till*, on *the Dow* (the Tao), its allusions to Ecclesiastes,

King Lear, and the country proverb about corn, its outrageous images of bluejay soccer fans and shameless exhibitionist shrubbery, this poem is an example of vigorous legpulling. If its moralizing sounds too bumptious for musical content, it can only remind us of passages in Beethoven or Haydn where certain effects seem a touch too literal for their context in the whole. I am thinking of Haydn's "Bear" and "Drumroll" symphonies, for instance, and of some of the tempest sounds in Beethoven's Sixth.

But a modern composer like Charles Ives would revel in the thought of all these themes sounded at once, jarring against each other with jocular energy, a collision of theme, motif, consonance, dissonance, and sheer noise. In poetry as in music, bewilderment can be fun if mounted correctly and managed just so.

What is necessary for "Each in His Season" to work is the situation outlined in an unrelated poem, "Venus and the Lute Player." There a swift allusion describes the ideal relationship of polyphonic variations to their underlying theme as being so natural and easy to perform that these variations seem inevitable, as when in lute music we find "whole notes, *cantus firmus,* implicit / In the tablature." That is to say, when the basic theme is perfectly agreeable to the instrument's arrangement of strings and frets variations seem to arise as if by their own accord. Now and again, though, the didacticism of "Each in His Season" pulls its *cantus firmus* (the description of seasonal nature) out of shape.

Yet the sequence is successful as a whole and it is but fitting to celebrate that success with a look at "Summer Sequence, iv." Here the theme of aggression is broached and the images chosen to represent it are the territorial combats of orioles, Ruby-throat hummingbirds, and purple buntings. The variations that this theme and accompanying imagery innervate are the inevitable ones of human warfare and of the accompanying industrialism that supplies it. Here, then, is the basic theme, its *cantus firmus* statement, and the accompanying variations.

The poetic form is a nervous free verse with two or three sharp accents per line. Staccato spondees abound, as do percussive internal rhymes and alliterations. Abrupt caesurae irregularly interrupt swift flights. The arrangement of the lines, their inden-

tations and hyphenated endings, suggests the to-and-fro skirmishes of the birds. The line "blue, blue, blue" streaks by like
the bunting it describes, and in the passage where hummingbirds
battle like fighter planes in a dogfight the pronouns "each" are
stacked in a way that illustrates spatial position:

> birds climb each
> 　　　above each other.

With its twentieth-century imagery and its sounds reminiscent
of Gerard Manley Hopkins, this poem makes to my ear a music
more like Stravinsky's than Vivaldi's. But it is genuine music
and few poets other than W. D. Snodgrass would ever attempt
anything like it. Almost none could bring it off:

> As cock orioles lock
> 　　　beaks and, orange
> 　　　　　slash-and-dart wings
> battering, flail the sky;
> 　　　as flyweight fighter-
> 　　　　　pilot, laser-
> throated humming-
> 　　　birds climb each
> 　　　　　above each other
> then dive down, drive
> 　　　each other off; fierce,
> 　　　　　piercing as the arc
> of an acetylene torch,
> 　　　or the hand-struck
> 　　　　　spark that might
> ignite and scorch the eye,
> 　　　here the buck bunting,
> 　　　　　indigo, his million
> prisms scattering
> 　　　shattered white light
> 　　　　　blue, blue, blue
> homes in through
> 　　　the startled air,
> 　　　　　a tracer or some
> riled-up, forge-
> 　　　bright rivet
> 　　　　　to its mark.

A Poet for All Seasons

BERNARD BENSTOCK

JUDGING A BOOK BY ITS COVER HAS BEEN A HOUSEHOLD PROCEDURE AT least since the demise of the scroll and the obsolescence of the papyrus page, and some books in the essentials invite such preliminary evaluation. The back cover of *Each in His Season*—to read the enveloping texts in reverse order, allowing for a progression from a "fixed" impression to a portraiture in a state of flux—features a photographic image of W. D, Snodgrass, an illumined face against a black backdrop. A prophet's beard, a patrician's nose, a scholar's spectacled eyes, a domed forehead, and a mouth caught in the act of self-expression foreshadow a volume of poems that is self-revealingly personal at certain moments, erudite and even arcane at others, lofty and caustic, and, at times, declamatory. Yet the slight twinkle of the veiled eyes also suggests various possibilities for outrageous mirth and malicious teasing.

The painting on the facing cover, on the other hand, is as bright and spontaneous as the black-and-white photograph is somber, DeLoss McGraw's artwork illustrative of the poetry rather than depictive of the poet. A young man's face in profile, composed of splashes of pastel colors, it also contains its prototypical origins in Archimboldo's *Primavera*—a set piece incorporating intimations of flowers and leaves and bird's wings—although the artist in this instance is also looking at Snodgrass's "Spring Suite" at the center of *Each in His Season*. The petals of hair seem to explode outward, spraying the dark background, while frail fragments and flakes fly about them, as if in illustration of fragments from the poet's "Dumbbell Rhymes":

> Hurl it sheer
> Twirling clear
> Past the planet's atmosphere

As a comet's kept in orbit
Till the earth's mass can absorb it.

McGraw's portraiture, like Snodgrass's poetry, insists both on a
fixed center and a constant whirling about of particles in Heracli-
tean transition. Greens and yellows and rusty shades of red
abound ("In clashing yellows, oranges, greens," the poet would
say), but the eyes, nose, throat, and mouth are distinctly outlined
in that poet's own dominant color, blue: "My lute's sky-blue as
a sky could be / And shaded out toward infinity." Or, as from the
"Summer Sequence," with a

million
prisms scattering
shattered white light
blue, blue, blue. . . .

Yet, since nothing in Snodgrass's poems ever retains its fixed
face value but performs multiple services often in conflicting
circumstances, blue also identifies the evil woman archetype
who announces, "My face is true cool blue," lending a sense of
androgyny to McGraw's Primavera.

The poet's basic statement regarding his craft (and sullen art),
among many in the collection, appears in "The Drunken Minstrel Rags His Bluegrass Lute," as he lays claim to the mantle
handed down by Wallace Stevens, that master of the Blue Guitar—one of many in the pantheon Snodgrass invokes by allusion.
The poem is a conflicted dialogue between a disgruntled public
and the defending minstrel, replete with echoes from such musical disparates as Jellyroll Morton ("I dreamed I heard all them
people say"), Simon and Garfunkel ("Mama don't 'llow no guitar
pickin' in here") and "Greensleeves" ("Bluegrass was all my
joy"). The minstrel is accused of salaciousness ("Blue movie
music"), as well as indifference ("under a cold blue moon"), and
told to color his instrument in almost any shade but blue. The
philistinic accusations are legion—obscurity, obscenity, "un-
mentionable" subject matter and "mixed up genres," immorality
and foreignness—and the poet hurls them all back, maintaining
his aloofness from the mob and denouncing the "blue stockings
and their cool blue laws." Building upon Dylan Thomas's declaration that his poems were written "for lovers, their arms / Round

the griefs of the ages," his successor cites his own inamorata as
the only fit object for his art:

> Blue gives my world the hue it has
>
> So for my high-toned song, I smugly
> Smuggle in all things vile and ugly
>
> To serenade my village Venus.
> Nothing else blue can come between us.

And as a final fillip he adds: "I jams true blue and dat's da trut'."
(An earlier poem, "Venus and the Lute Player," sets the stage for
the lady and her troubadour.)

Like Penelope, Snodgrass unravels everything he weaves in
order to reweave within new patterns and frames, which makes
a collection like this recent one far more than the sum total of
its poetic parts (some old, most new, nothing borrowed, decid-
edly blue). In the last verse of the "Spring Suite" the shades of
blue are catalogued and reevaluated in the process:

> Now robins' eggs betray the hue
> Of Andrew Marvell's drop of dew
> Reflecting heaven and Mary's cloak of blue
>
> Clear as some super-Aryan eye
> Bright with its vision of a sky
> Where nestlings scramble up to fly
> Dogfights for wealth and mastery by and by.

Warfare imagery saturates Snodgrass's poems, and his clear blue
sky is frequently the battle area for fighter planes as well as birds.
The blue mists that he spirals throughout the poems also have
their green counterparts—another facet of the poet himself—
perhaps invocative of lost innocence to balance the songs of blue
experience—and at times identified with another innocent victim and old friend, Cock Robin, the "robin with green face."

Just as the tulip first manifests itself as "tight green buds /
like fists," in his "translation" of Lorca, Snodgrass commands
summer greenness into existential being: "Green: we're eager for
you, green; / The garden gone green; green for Go." The mechanical nature of the traffic signal augments and undercuts the or-

ganic process of nature, and metaphors of finance and patriotism
become dominant factors in the process, as the tree

> bends to green's rule and currency,
> finding somewhere some shred or rag
> of green to hang out for a flag.

The last stanza repeats the opening line with a vengeance
("Green; we're greedy for you, green"), the profusion of summer
fecundity threatening to overwhelm the natural process, "the
bankroll buying out the bank." Soon after in the "Sequence,"
as "deregulated summer rolls on," "the greenback reigns"—the
world of finance, like many another aspect of the materialist
world, is never far from the natural world as dreamed of in the
poet's philosophy.

As a portfolio of poems, a diversified portfolio, *Each in His
Season* is also a palimpsest of poems, the book title deriving
from the middle section of five (the four sequences of "Each in
His Season"), and only the last section of nine poems ("in
Flower") replicates the natural world of seasonal changes, significantly that of springtime. Of the others, "The Midnight Carnival" and "Dance Suite, Et Alia" carry quite a different burden,
while the opening "Birds Caught, Birds Flying" navigates somewhat between the confines of nature and the domain of the
world, the flesh and the devil—as well as the poet. For Snodgrass
the natural world is almost invariably the starting point, the origins of things, the basis for possibility, but nature rarely succeeds
in withstanding the encroachment of the manmade universe. The
language in which everything is couched suffers the same fate:
the lyrical is quickly dissolved into the colloquial: technical
terms and slang, popular idioms and expletives, the vernacular
that Stephen Dedalus identifies as "the language of the market-
place." Snodgrass is relentless in making an almost immediate
compromise with the debased, his language reflecting the mirror
imagery in which the exalted is inevitably reduced to defilement.
The procedure is reversed, however, in "W.D.'s Carnival Friends":

> I saw a pig with a tambourine;
> A Satanical wolf with a snout of green,
> His teeth bared, glittering and obscene.

An angel hovered above this scene
Whose eyes were closed and his smile serene.

The "real" world consists of finance, commerce, industry, the
technology of gadgets and appliances and automobiles, domes-
ticity, warfare, pollution and crime and rock music, medicine
and psychiatry—each of which provides its own adaptable vocabulary for "things vile and ugly."

The military metaphor—again aeronautical—dominates the
summer mating of birds, as their

> slash-and-dart wings,
> battering, flail the sky;
> as flyweight fighter-
> pilot, laser-
> throated humming-
> birds climb each
> above each other
> then dive down, drive
> each other off.

Autumn provides its own skirmishes, since

> Sharp, black crickets
> have got the house
> surrounded; miners and sappers
> gnaw our siding,

and "The wind's war / Moves up closer." Winter (in "Snow
Songs") completes a military maneuver that began so hopefully
in Spring; so that now

> Bones, like the broken branches,
> soften, sink back down
> in ground that sent them
> out to reconnoitre.
> Soon this whole, broad
> Stalingrad will be no more
> than scattered fading photographs,
> just some aging soldiers'
> recollections.

When spring returns, and flowers begin to bloom, the metaphor accelerates: dandelions are hailed by "intermittent snip-

ing," until "the broad yard erupts / in small arms fire," while peonies are spotted by "a tracer scoring / the night sky, uplifting / buds still sheathed," a flowering forth as "the rocket bursts / full flower heads on the abyss, / in a rush of fresh blood." Longfellow's view of Nature as "red in tooth and claw" pales besides Snodgrass's, whose perspective is clinically Darwinian. The struggle for survival results in an aggrandizement that even involves such nonferal items as in the vegetable world:

> Battling for the sun, young ash
> and maples take up the choice
> locations, shading their neighbors out.

The animal world follows suit, with even greater potential for ferociousness ("Both crow and owl devour / each other's young"), all in the name of survival. The fury of the metaphor increases to include a kind of "natural" imperialism when

> swarms of convict colonists
> and outcasts spread across the land.
> Nestlings shrilling to be fed, the roughnecks
> flourish, the smaller or more timid
> are never much missed.

When the vernal season is over, the "leading colonists of summer, / Carriers of what we called progress" head south, "taking their plunder" with them.

The technological appurtenances of war have their analogue in the gadgetry of peace, although even bumper car drivers in a festive carnival are militantly alerted into action with: "Kamakazi pilots, man your planes!" In the natural world the narcissus is like a "yellow Deco / telephone" and the dandelions are disseminated by "a spook transmitter." The human world is comprised of "acetylene desires" and the voice of the departed loved one "can overload our circuits," while the quest for one's soul— which begins in surgical terms—becomes a matter of "dismantling / computers to reach / a text." Nor are these occasional metaphors and similes only sporadic occurrences—an entire poem concerning the "forces of love" that the persona hopes to recapture is patterned as a set of numbered operating instructions for assembling an apparatus ("The Forces of Love Reassem-

ble W. D.: Instructions"); the dancers in "Hip Hop" are "wind
up toys," "rapping like a robot," a "mannikin or clone," "a tall
doll / rigid and mechanical"; and one suspects that "Dumbbell
Rhymes" narrates the machinations of manipulating a pinball
machine that evolves into a meteoric parallel in the heavens,

> Twirling clear
> Past the planet's atmosphere
> As a comet's kept in orbit.

Where technology thrives, can the industrial world be far behind? The summer insects

> grind on
> Like the whirr where distant foundries
> Work all three shifts,

and the winter sky is "God's bobbin mills," and even love is
assembled (and disassembled) on an assembly line. "Cock
Robin's Escape from the Alizarin of Evening" has the bird
"zing" into

> the vast blast furnace,
> Into the mottled, clotted-blood-black cauldron roiling factory
> smoke and flame,
> Into the mill foundry,

which quickly evolves into an alchemical formula, in "midnight's crucible and corona."

Each in His Season carries no explicit critique of the military-
industrial complex, dependence on faddish technology, or the
excesses of late capitalism, but deploys the language of these
characteristics of contemporary American society to tease and
even taunt, the vocabulary of our consumer culture acting as self-
denigration. Only two poems announce themselves as carrying
political weight: "Elena Ceauçescu's Bed" mockingly poses the
existence of the executed Romanian's bed as a sort of tourist
attraction ("Making ourselves at home in that broad bed / Elena
left"), so as to challenge the smugness of political indifference
to the "homeless and hungering" and the displaced native
Americans "who hunted, once, that hill where my house stands";

the other, "The Ballad of Jesse Helms," deliberate doggerel to lampoon the self-proclaimed arbiter of moral righteousness—and if predecessors Hitler and Stalin are included in the lambasting, it is under their original names of "Schicklgruber and Djugashvili." Particles from this broad satire pepper many of the poems, adding a linguistically political dimension rather than specific political themes. A minute dissection of the body politic, however, does occur in another poem that masquerades as an ode "In Memory of Lost Brain Cells," but the "drunken / Purge [that] wipes out our cells" are the political purges that result in thought control, cowardice and desertions, and a lack of political awareness:

> those connections
> They formed live on in spite of past defections,
>
> In spite of new betrayals, quislings, quitters.
> Others fill in, take up where old transmitters
>
> Shut down.

Not since W. H. Auden refined the art of the elliptical innuendo along quasi-political lines has the most innocent of commodities been filtered through so political a sieve as in Snodgrass's fine-grinding, where an autumnal drabness is seen as

> The few birds left accept
> the mob opinions
> and the fashions: a dull
> Stalinist grey that will
> offend no one.

The somber poems of "Autumn Variations" are devoid of many variables, mostly focusing on loss and absence and even desolation:

> Imperial greenery withdraws,
> flamboyant and corrupt; the leaf's
> far government's lost
> faith in its mission, that certainty
> to be despotic and
> victorious.

Only winter reverses the march toward totalitarianism as everything is covered with forgetfulness "under the soft, featureless / democracy of snow." But it is the politico-linguistics that emerges as the dominant factor in whatever social concerns are transmitted, with the "Tattooed Man" a walking repository of slogans, headlines, shibboleths, captions, cryptic messages, obiter dicta, labels, incantations, stock phrases, graffiti, advertisements, and writings on the wall, which include "allusive Pisan cantos" and messages on "Nazi lampshades."

Snodgrass uses words like bullets, as much for their percussive effects as for their impact and penetration, and the constant sniping detected from the peripheries suggests an ongoing war of nerves, as well as a battle of the sexes. While on occasion his persona stands aside as an observer of a Miltonic battle in heaven,

> You are yourself who stands aside
> To watch and witness, petrified,
> While vast universal powers collide
> In archetypal conflict to decide
> Whether good fortune or ill betide,

more often he finds himself engaged in a domestic tiff. The opening poem, "Anniversary Verses for My Oldest Wife," concedes that conflicts have ended and all losses are restored, although the sentiment is cloaked in a touch of ironic bravado: "This new dog's learned the right / Old dame can fix you fast." Shifting the scene in "A Curse" to that of a targeted enemy, one "who does not make instruments" (although apparently must have promised to do so), the long malediction ends with

> Every midnight may you lie
> Awake with one who'll scorn and rule
> You for a coward and a fool.
> That is, I hope you spend your life
> Alone—or better, with your wife.

Distancing the domestic discontent away from home nonetheless focuses relentlessly on the subject of the botched marriage, and the "Human Torch" in Snodgrass's Midnight Carnival bridges the span between lover and husband in his reference to his "lady love, trim in her green / Short skirt—my other ball and chain."

The teasing tone of these versions of the marital engagement gives way in such poems as "Birds Caught, Birds Flying" to a pained ambivalence: love leaving suggests a freedom of flight, yet the implications throughout are of love *locked-in*, of empty houses containing the corpses of love. The departing "lover" soon becomes the betrayer, as in the third poem of the "Pretexts" series which focuses not only on "Your one love [who] left you impassed and alone," but also on the "best friend" with whom she departed, a replay in bitter tones of Shakespeare's sonnet sequence. Love is rarely sublime for long, but quickly moves to the erotic and even the debased:

> one chance to
> > romance her,
> one hand's in
> > her pants, sir,
> progressing through fixed patterns to the
> pulse of love's low Art.

or, as the medley of "Various 1930s Love Songs" concludes:

> They dream in vain, in the bowels it will remain
> Like a leaf that's caught in the tide
>
> Or the drain
>
> While many a lying lover's lain
> In back rooms and dark hallways.

The culprit invariably is the heartless seductress, in one instance portrayed as a rich, underaged vamp in "A Teen-Ager" and immediately after a former love in "An Old Flame," obviously still manipulative at long distance. "Masquerada" in particular sets up the sexual power play in a dialogue of seduction with each of the protagonists ("He" and "She") jockeying for power, attempting to determine the rules, and violating any presumed regulations ("Each one's reaching below the belt"). Although "He" takes pride in his virility ("I project in place-. / A red-hot poker face"), "She" presents the most chilling statement of empowerment: "I circle like a shark." The various personifications of the She in these poems lead to a particularly familiar character, the Miss Treavle who appears in "Mr. Evil Disguises Himself as Herself—with Murder in Her heart for W. D." and later reprises in a poem of her own, "Apache: Miss Treavle Pursues W. D."

In her first guise she arrives as a stripteaser in a melodic verse that traces her body lithely down the page as a descriptive process, "arrows pointing / to the crotch." Description gives way in the third stanza to pronouncement (a familiar technique in several of the poems), identifying her as the archetypal seductress:

> Time to welcome our Miss Treavle,
> Shaped with all some daughter of Eve'll
> > give
> > a man,
> > then when
> > she's had 'im,
> Drive him forth, stripped
> > stark as Adam.

It is with the seduced Adam that the poetic persona identifies— perhaps with the killed Cock Robin as well—as Mr. Evil waltzes through this succession of poems as Miss Treavle's instigator (his other self) and Cock Robin's murderer. As she pursues the personified W. D. through the apache dance, there are multiple facets to her personality rendering her both ingratiating and infuriating, coy and aggressive, hesitant and relentless. "Don't give up on little Me," she pleads, admitting that she's "rotten" and will "desert you, / Hurt you, / Then do you dirt, too," but is somewhat introspective as to her motives. Having been treated by a "shrink," she judges herself cured ("He thinks I'm better"), and while conceding that "You / Ought to leave me like the rest," returns of course to her alluring demeanor:

> You won't be cruel;
> You will
> Find that I'm your jewel.

Finally, in "Tap Dance: W. D. Escapes from Miss Treavle," the announced escape ("fresh out of love, / I could jump jail walls"), is constantly undercut by the italicized lines that follow each stanza and eventually group together as the poem's envoi, highlighting the escapee's presence within the confines still of sexual slavery, the "groin slaves."

These "paradise lost" poems in the "Dance Suite" vary the familiar dramatis personae, isolating at times W. D., Mr. Evil (a.k.a. Miss Treavle), and Cock Robin—in a kaleidoscopic pattern allowing for a certain potential for role-changing. "Through the flaming gates of Eden" Evil/Treavle undergoes a transvestitic "exchange" leading into a transsexual "something rare and sex-strange," now "Sleek as an cobra / steeped in venom," now "lithe as an adder." The Serpent in the Garden takes on its particular importance in "W. D. Sees Himself Animated" in conflict with the robin. The persona is a three-year-old infant when the "sneaky snake" appears to him in the form of a "fine new toy / That brightens the peaceful nursery," the fierce bird engaging the serpent in an epic battle before the child's eyes, the snake now identified as the bird's "serpentine / Brother and foe." The "serpent, sleek and wily," vies for control of the "innocent stupid child," himself inanimate and apparently controlled in a predetermined battle while passively waiting "in the wings." No meek robin, this "broadwinged, brilliant feathered bird" is victorious in its allegorical struggle, rescuing the child from "malignant forces" and revealing its particular power "To fill our skies, like creation's word, / With songs such as mortals never heard," so that the child emerges as poet, harlequined with one red hand and foot and one green hand and foot, standing on his own two feet and declaring: "I speak for the bird who sang for me." The epic struggle determines the essence of the artist in an escape from the world/flesh/devil into art.

The preexisting existential question as to "Who Killed Cock Robin?" allows for few ambiguities (he is dead and has certainly been murdered), but Snodgrass replays the possible circumstances in several ways, effecting a resurrection myth from his reconstruction. His Robin (the "Cock of the Waking") has titular presence in four poems in the "Dance Suite, Inter Alia," as well as an important unnamed role in a fifth—in which "W. D. Sees Himself Animated" (i.e., as Robin). The Cock Robin narrative begins when the feminized Mr. Evil deflects W. D.'s thoughts away from the bird; "a yellow skirt that ghosts down the / hallways of the heart," she seductively wraps "her arms around my ears where sweet / birdsong once would start," interfering with poetic creativity. In his masculine guises Mr. Evil, to W. D.'s horror, attempts to throttle or abscond with the bird:

> Turn
> That
> Red-
> Breast
> Loose
>   before I faint, sir;

but, although at first pusillanimous in his rescue attempt ("How can I face this abduction?"), W. D. gathers strength and orders Evil out of town, "fierce and defiant" in his challenge:

> Set
> That
> Bird
>   Down
> and that's an order.

Yet, the image of the lost Cock Robin troubles him as it affects his own ability to create his birdsongs, and "The Memory of Cock Robin Dwarfs W.D." concludes in a mournful note:

> Still, if that voice that overjoyed
>   me were destroyed,
>   the void
>   would make me shrink
>   to think
> and never shape one note or word
>   matching that bird
>   once heard.

(The artistry is in the *shaping*, as the coda-poem of the suite, "To Shape a Song," testifies). Cock Robin does manage to escape, breaking out of his own traumas of birth in Whitmanesque magnificence ("Out of the eggshell, fearlessly rocketting"), but more importantly out of the love-trap—the snare set up by the seductress, "Out of Love's capitalism, the four-square caged and cornered market / Where value lies in scarcity, virtue in poverty and the payoff sucks," till it *zings* into "midnight's crucible and corona," "robbed of self-fakery, robed in *bel canto's* naked and complete steel," where it undoubtedly contributes to the creation of "The Midnight Carnival" section of Snodgrass's collection.

Few poets are as multivalent in their styles as W. D. Snodgrass, who has long abandoned the modernist poet's insistence on developing a single dominant voice, opting instead in so diversified a poetic portfolio as to keep the reader listening carefully for the distinctiveness of the *poem's* voice. That other modernist credo, therefore—that each piece of art determines its own shape, form, style—is religiously adhered to, creating a diversity of unique proportions. The prevailing characteristic of multiple and internal rhymes so overwhelms the volume that the five unrhymed poems early in the first section seem, in retrospect, to be anomalies, yet the fixed line lengths (themselves anomalous) make them appear so obviously different from what we would assume to be free verse. The lyric qualities of the nature poems, with the uninflected tones of violence, provide them with one sort of consistency in style, while the initiating section contains an amorphous grouping of narratives ("The girl outside your window . . ."; "The Sealchie's Son", "Love Lamp"), mood pieces ("As a Child, Sleepless"; "Venus and the Lute Player"), and a semi-narrative with heightened mood ("Birds Caught, Birds Flying"). These in turn are immediately followed by a set of caustic verses, instructive, even didactic and vituperative, eighteenth-century in their satirical thrust and Audenesque in their clinical incisiveness (especially the four experimental villanelles under the umbrella title of "Pretexts")—only to be overturned by the outrageous doggerel of "The Ballad of Jesse Helms."

"The Midnight Carnival" provides another frame for quasi-narrative, mainly vernacular, character-dominated ("W. D.'s Carnival Friends"—including a "baby dressed like a cutthroat gnome"—the "Wire Walker," the "Human Torch," the "Tattooed Man," "Dr. P.H.D. Dark, Hypnotist," "The Carnival Girl," "The Strolling Minstrel" and "The Drunken Mistrel," as well as the barker of the "House of Horrors"). A Bakhtinian feast of grotesques (bracketed by "The Capture of Mr. Sun" and "The Capture of Mr. Moon"), they conjure up a world that is profane, at times predetermined and at other times indeterminate, depleted, apocalyptic, immune to change, "out of style," visceral, and almost always precarious. The most positive note, however—perhaps the only upbeat note in the entire "carnival"—is the insistence of the drunken minstrel on the efficacy of his art ("My country chords stand resolute. / Discord and dat makes a blue-grass lute").

Evocative of that other midnight carnival, the Circean nighttown in Joyce's *Ulysses*, Snodgrass's is a constant procession of metamorphoses, a world continuously changing but remaining abysmally unaffected by change. The caged lion is a sun, a sunflower, a flower "tracing / the sun on its rounds," and cyclically a lion: "we shiver / at his smile, his frown." The Tattooed Man presents a plethora of messages, but the languages change (English, Italian, Latin, Classical Greek, transliterated Hebrew) and the cumulative "meanings" disintegrate into near-gibberish, resulting in the overwhelming question, "does heat bring out new sentences / and my old syntax changes?" The dumbbell rhymes tumble over each other in trip-hammer profusion, yet inevitably lead to atrophy: "That's enough now, I'm exhausted." The hypnotist drains energy from the subject's brain, and although proclaiming himself as "your mentor, priest, / your lover," fails to induce the intended awakening—even love fails to energize, "wanting warmth," "light / lacking, locked affections." The bumper cars careen through a maze of warnings, heeding no warning, doomed on a collision course, and each looking glass in the Hall of Mirrors reflects negation, "a shrouded / face and history," the pursuer "who / 's gaining on you," the loss of individuality: "This turns you to a multitude / of shouting clones." It seems that history is to blame, as the House of Horrors attests:

> and it gets hard to tell it from
> Versailles' vast Hall of Mirrors
> where cataclysmic peace broke out;
> as if the polished granite pillars of
> burnt Persepolis gave back your face,
> the walls of Altamira your nickname
> and secret vices; as if the air
> held all sound waves created
> since the first big bang.

The supreme tour de force of the volume are the nineteen poems of "Dance Suite, Inter Alia," ten of which have "suggested" melodies attached as instructional notes, their preexisting tunes driving the rhythmic forces of the verses. The first, to Beethoven's Minuet in G, is deceptive, the stately pace presumably inappropriate for the sexual (although initially rather coyly sexual) intentions, but coyness blithely shifts into a more overt movement: "Guide that deep-sighed, sloe-eyed, sly coquette- / Don't just sweat: Minuet." (The title ignores the composer's key for a more bawdy, if bowdlerized, "Minuet in F♯.") Bawdiness surfaces again and again, as when the designated melody is "The Stripper" or the "common 'apache' dance," but melody of course is only an excuse—the intimacy of the couple locked together in the dance offers the operative possibilities. They fox-trot to "Whispering" and waltz to "Tales of the Vienna Woods," execute a Mexican Hat Dance to *Jurape Tapatio* and a tango to *La Cumparsita*, and the poetics down the printed page keep step to the specific fancy footwork (e.e. cummings traced a leaf falling down the page and tracked a grasshopper up-and-down it; Snodgrass is as graphically pointillist when the scheme demands, his opening spring poem "expanding" as the developing season insinuates itself, from an opening line of two short words to a final line of nine longer ones).

The Latin songs in particular lend themselves to a frenetic beat that determines all aspects of rhythm, tone, spacing, diction, and rhyme, with their strongly suggestive sexual undertones. The hat dance pounds itself out in stiletto heels to conclude:

> So take off all these helmets, quixotic,
> Or you'll turn a pyrotic neurotic,
> Patriotic, narcotic, hypnotic, despotic,
>   Idiotical con-or per-vert

—in other words, erotic. Others are pure pastiche, as in "Medley: Mortal Love Watches the Dance," where the indicated melody is a multitude, assorted love songs of the thirties, "That Old Black Magic," "The Music Goes Round and Round," "Sunday, Monday, and Always," "For All We Know," "Dancing in the Dark," and "Stardust." (In a momentary digression of ecumenical harmonizing pop music blends with high culture: "For all they know they may never meet again / In thunder, lightning, spite or rain.")

As these tunes suggest, Snodgrass delights in playing parodic games, with Shakespearean lines as well as those written by Hoagy Carmichael, but nowhere as pronounced as in the Dance Suite. Occasional fragments echo Whitman and Lorca, Auden and Eliot, with hints of Frost and cummings and William Carlos Williams and Dylan Thomas, some quite obvious in the fortissimo, others mere hints pianissimo. Shakespeare and T. S. Eliot—a coupling Eliot himself had instigated—nudge each other on occasion, as in the third autumnal variation, where the desolations of the season are examined: "it cannot come to good. / . . . on the bare ground, litter / and stub ends." Eliot's Shakespeherian Rag is reprised in "The Carnival Girl Darkly Attracts W. D.," which begins with

> O she does teach the torches to burn bright
> As a rich jewel in an Ethiop's ear.
> Romeo,
> Romeo,
> Ro'me o-ver
> In the clo-ver
> Besides, what would I say to her?
> *Belle qui tient ma vie* . . .

The overwhelming result in *Each in His Season* is that W. D. Snodgrass soberly walks a straight line while drunkenly careening in many directions, capturing so much of the phenomenal world while gliding in and out of the sublime as well.

Snodgrass Underground: An Interview

BRENDA TREMBLAY

BT: How did people react to the publication of the first cycle of Bunker poems in 1977?

WDS: Many reacted terribly. I could say that it has ruined my career in certain ways. I have been called a pro-Nazi which is absolutely absurd. I have said worse things about the Nazis than any historian has said. Once, after a reading I had given, a man stood up and said, "How dare you glorify these people." Well, fortunately, I didn't have to say anything; the rest of the audience sort of rose up in wrath and beat that idea down. Then, he wrote to me but had now changed his accusation to, "You have humanized them." Well, I'm sorry. I'm an atheist, but my answer to that is you can't blame me for what God did. You know, they are human, and if you don't want to admit that, then I think you don't want to admit that you share some of their qualities, and I think that's very dangerous.

BT: What do you expect the reception will be for the completed cycle?

WDS: I don't know. I mean, of course, I've worried about this a great deal. It could quite recover people's opinion of me; it could just strengthen them in thinking I'm a no-good S.O.B; it could do both, which is more likely. So far, the reception has been quite lovely. I just heard from Al Poulin (the publisher of *The Fuehrer Bunker*) the other night that Roget Asselineau had given it a very good review in France and that feels very good to me. In general, it has been much better received in Europe than it has here.

BT: Why do you suppose that is?

WDS: I think because they had a direct experience of the Nazis, whereas here the Nazis are mostly figures of people's fantasy life. For example, one of the people who has been most enthusiastic is a Pole named Leszek Szaryga who we met not too long ago and who translated all of Magda Goebbels's poems, maintaining

105

the incredibly complicated verse forms. All of her poems use forms from French love poems partly because sex was one of her chief weapons and partly because, you know, the thing about romantic love is to tell the big lie—that I care more about you than I care about me. Hogwash! But, you know, you tell the big lie and you keep telling it often enough and people believe it, they buy it, so I thought okay, that's like what we do in politics. You tell them, we're doing this for your benefit, so you've got to come in the army and go kill a bunch of people over in so-and-so where we want markets.

BT: You've been working on these poems for a long time.

WDS: A long time, say about thirty-five years, at least. In a sense I've been working on the Bunker since the end of World War II. I started to write a play based on Trevor Roper's *The Last Days of Hitler,* and that didn't work, but I stayed interested in it as everybody else did, and I guess since then a lot of people have tried to write plays and movies about it. At that time, that seemed terrible to a lot of people to try to do that. Since then it has seemed terrible to people that I write poems about it. There's more prose written about this subject since the war than probably anything except dieting—or cooking. Cookbooks and dieting and then Nazi history.

BT: Is the bunker still there?

WDS: Yes and no. I tried to get there once, but was immediately surrounded by two jeeps full of East German soldiers, and almost got shot.

BT: It's a no-man's-land, isn't it?

WDS: Yes, and it's right beside the border, next to the Berlin Wall. Fortunately, I was wearing a bright white leather raincoat, so it was clear I wasn't trying to sneak around or trying to escape over the wall which was part of the reason you were liable to get shot. At that time, you couldn't get into the bunker anyway; the Russians had filled it full of gasoline and burned it and then water got in and started destroying a lot of it. But nowadays they are digging in that area and putting up beautiful hotels of all sorts; at least when I was there three or four years ago, magnificent luxury hotels and things like this. They're coming up with all sorts of parts of the bunker they hadn't known existed. Apparently the whole underground was like groundhog holes everywhere and there were all kind of bunkers under there. We had known there was one higher up where Magda Goebbels and her children stayed at the end, whereas Hitler and Goebbels were in the lowest bunkers. But they're coming up with old uniforms, and with papers they thought didn't exist, records and things of that sort.

One of the things, this is kind of interesting, that they're building there is a theater, and there was a German theater director who wanted to do a performance of the Bunker poems; you know, this has been done as a stage performance from time to time. He was going to have it translated into German, and he wanted to present it on the site where the real bunker had been. This really scared me blue. I mean, up to now I have felt that however much other people said I was doing something immoral, I knew I was not and I felt quite sure. What I wasn't so sure of was what effect a presentation might have on the neo-Nazis. I mean, I could get shot by a liberal or a neo-Nazi or a moderate. I could get shot by anybody. Still, that wasn't what I was really worried about. I was worrying whether or not this was a good thing to do or not.

BT: So we continue to learn more about the bunker. But that raises an important question, I think, about historical perspective. What would you say—where did you draw the line between fact and speculation?

WDS: I've tried mostly to be very accurate historically. Sometimes there were things which later proved not to be true; for instance, it was said—it was thought—that Hitler during the last days had opened the floodgates from the lake and let the waters come into the subway system where many, many refugees, wounded people, old, old men and women living down there to get away from the air raids were all drowned. Well, it turns out that wasn't so, he didn't do that. But I have a long poem about it in here ["Adolph Hitler: 'Benito, pattern, partner, my brother . . .'"]. I haven't taken it out. It seems to me that it is so typical of what he did do. I mean try to understand what he was doing at the end of the war; he was trying to get as many people killed as he could, including, by then, particularly Germans, who he was furious with because they wouldn't make him master of the world. I think also he just wanted to be bigger in the history books, and the more people who sacrificed their lives for him, gave up their life for him, well, clearly, that was his obsession from the beginning—prove that you care more about my life than yours. So, it seemed to me that *that* was true in a way beyond fact. Just the fact that everyone believed it showed that there was a certain justice to that notion, so I've left it in. There are a couple of things like that, a couple of places where I have deliberately changed, shifted history around.

BT: And invented history?

WDS: Yes, with Himmler, for example, where I've invented something that didn't happen at all. Himmler was head of the SS and he wrote poems. In some of his poems a trainload of what were called *Lebensborn* children turns up. These were the illegitimate children of SS men. The SS were encouraged and their women were encouraged to have children, legitimate or illegitimate. Also, Himmler would take children stolen in the countries in the east because he decided that if they had blond hair and blue eyes they must really be Aryans; even if they were Jewish he would say that Aryan blood had gotten into the family. These children were to become sort of the prizefighters of the Reich when they were still thinking that they were going to have a thousand-year Reich. They were to be like the Janissaries under the Turks. They would be converted to this belief and they would never rise very high, they would never rise into total control, but they would live lives edging toward luxury. They would be sort of the prize specimens. Well, in my version ["Heinrich Himmler: 'ARYAN*PURITY*A*STRAIN'"] I had a trainload of them shipped accidentally to army headquarters about thirty miles south of Berlin. If you know the German train system, you know that couldn't happen. The German trains get to the places where they're supposed to be and they get there on time, even during wars. Well, that's a joke, you know; some of the trains did get fouled up under wartime conditions.

BT: But it was important for you to have some sense of veracity.

WDS: It seems to me that's one of the most awful things they did, steal these children. I wanted to get that in. And what Himmler is saying there, he's saying they musn't fall into the hands of our enemies, the Americans or the Russians, because if they find out we have stolen them from their parents and that they weren't thieves and prostitutes as we told them, they will want vengeance on us in twenty years and will do terrible things to us, so we must kill them now. Yeah, he wasn't a very nice man. So, I wanted to get his attitude in: if these children are going to fall into the hands of our enemies, kill them first. And I wanted to get that in, so I invented this thing that didn't happen. I invented some things for Speer because I wanted to show that he wasn't all as lovely as he said. Since then we have found other things that he has done, and if those had been known at the time, I would have used those, but instead I used the things I did use—and left them.

BT: You've said that the hardest person in the book for you to feel contact with was Hitler. What did you do to try to get into the mind-set of Hitler?

WDS: Just kept looking—just reading about his life and looking, trying to think why did he do this, what in his past was related to that. Now some people have said I'm trying to justify him, make some kind of Freudian justification for what he did based on things that happened in his childhood. I'm doing nothing of the sort. Many people suffered far worse things than he did as children and became quite decent people. That's a silly argument, but I've encountered it any number of times. They say I'm offering excuses for him. No, I'm not doing anything of the sort. If anything, I'm showing that from his earliest days he was rather maligned, and beyond being maligned he was incredibly egotistical and self-centered, far beyond almost anyone we can think of.

BT: Do you think he was crazy?

WDS: It depends on what you mean by crazy. He was crazy like a fox in certain ways. He knew how to sway people to his opinion. Everybody talks about the power of his eyes; he knew immediately in front of an audience—I've known people who were like this, not with audiences but with individuals, but he was like this with a group—that he would know right away what their fixations were, what their hatreds, and he could play on them instantly. He was really quite magical at that. He was also terribly good at memorizing small details about the armies, about the war, about everything of that sort. The thing was, he wasn't much good about strategy; he was good at tactics. He could perceive very early where his enemies—the French, the English, the Czechs—where they were greedy and cowardly and would back off. He knew how far he could go at every point. He also knew that they should not, in that first winter, retreat from Moscow, even though it cost terribly to stay there. But then that fixed itself into a solution for everything, and from then on it was, "no, we will not retreat." That so clearly wasn't working; he should have seen he was just getting more and more people killed. But, on the details, he could tell you exactly how many men were supposed to be in this unit, how many guns they had, how many tanks; at the end of the war, of course, this was all nonsense. It wasn't true anymore. I remember I asked Speer about this. I said, you know, look, you were there up to about four days from the end in the bunker and Hitler was again ordering these troops out to be killed, guys who'd been killed four times already. I mean how many times can you get that unit killed? How can he have been sending them out? He has to have known they were dead. Everybody else knew they were dead.

BT: What did Speer say?

WDS: He said that Hitler was like a friend of his in school who became a great cancer specialist, a marvelous diagnostician. He didn't even have to take tests, but would look at you and know whether you had cancer or not. He would run the tests anyway, but he already knew. He told us, Speer said, that he would die himself of cancer, but when he got it, he was the only one who didn't know. Then, Speer said something wonderful. He said, "he neglected his knowing." Man, I want to carve that on the wall because that's so much the truth about Hitler and what was awful about him, and it's also the truth about Speer. He neglected his knowing. He claims, you know, that he should have found out about the camps in the east, should have found out about. . . . Hogwash! He had a friend who came to him and said, "Don't find out what's happening in the camps in the east." That's enough, that tells you; you know what's happening when you're told that. You'd be better off *not* to know this.

BT: I read that Speer was called the "good Nazi," that people identified with him somehow, after the war was over.

WDS: Well, yeah, there's been a lot of argument about that. I interviewed him a long, long time ago; he's dead now. I found him a likable man in many ways. I didn't believe everything he was telling me, but, on the other hand, he was more honest than

most of the other Nazis would be, I thought. Also, that undoubtedly is the reason he wasn't executed. He also knew he hadn't
done such terrible things, and by repentance he could probably
save his life, which he did. I think you can question his sincerity
in his repentance. It's a very questionable thing. It's a question
to me whether you can be that high in the Nazi government, any
government, without having done a fair number of filthy things,
which he had. But he was more honest about it than most. He
was a very intelligent man, also, which no doubt helped his case.
Joe Persico, a friend of ours down in Mexico who has just brought
out a book about the Nuremberg trials, gets very upset that some
of the other people were executed and Speer wasn't. Well, I'm
inclined to think it made sense. In some ways he was sort of a
redeemable person. When I interviewed him at his ancestral
home on the hill above Heidelberg, where right across the street,
practically, was the beautiful old castle and right down the road
was the American commanding general of all our forces, I said,
"Don't you think it's a little strange that you're living here right
next . . . ," and he said, "Yeah, it's very strange, but they stare
even more when I have lunch with Elie Wiesel, the famous Nazi
hunter. I had lunch with him recently in Vienna and am cooper-
ating with his people."

BT: So, at times, what made you not believe him?

WDS: Oh, I was pretty sure you can't be that pure and be that
high in the Nazi government. I must say that his book [*Inside
the Third Reich*], which is full of mea culpa and breastbeating,
didn't quite convince me, and there was something in the tone
that was too—oily. Also, I asked him in my interview, I said, you
know what interests me about this so much is that we don't know
of any other time when there's been so much betrayal in a small
compass. No doubt there has been in the Kremlin, but we don't
have any of their records. Since then I would have said that sort
of thing has happened in Washington too, but there are eighteen-
minute gaps! I said that you say in your book that with your
family's liberal background that for you to join the Nazi party
was a betrayal. And what did you get, all those other betrayals
happening, one after another, especially among the high Nazis
there inside the bunker and during the last days. And he said,
"Well, that's true, it's true that it was a betrayal of my family. On

the other hand, think of the position I was in. I was a young man, I was an architect, I wanted to build, I couldn't build anything. All of a sudden I was given the opportunity to build everything in the country." He said, "You know, I don't think even my father could have resisted that." I thought, okay, that's the real man talking. It says, yeah, that was rotten. It was a terrible thing to do, but who could resist?

BT: I think he was flattered by the attention at the time, from what I've read.

WDS: You mean the attention from Hitler. Oh, yes, of course, certainly. The man was able to work a kind of magic over people that's quite astonishing. And generally speaking, the women were interested first. That was why, for instance, he couldn't marry Eva Braun. That's part of the reason; he had to keep that appeal to the women in the audience. In a great many of the families, the women went over to him first, and then they converted the family. That happened with Eva Braun's family.

BT: What about Eva Braun? What was her relationship with Hitler?

WDS: Eva Braun had many small revenges against Hitler for his neglect of her. Also, she couldn't have the kinds of things that she wanted. She came from a very conventional Catholic family, wanted marriage, children, and also she would like to have been able to be present at the great state dinners to be recognized as the mistress of the great dictator. Instead, she had to pose as a secretary, and then, on top of that, he really didn't pay much attention to her. He didn't think much of her, of women. He said, "One should have a stupid woman. One is better off that way. She doesn't get in your way and prevent your doing what you feel like doing." Among her revenges for this kind of thing was keeping two nasty little dogs. He kept one big German shepherd called, of course, Blondi. She kept two nasty little scotties that yelped and bounced all over the place and bit people and misbehaved and whatnot. She also went on asking for American movies after it was no longer patriotic to do so. All the Nazis were terribly fond of American movies, especially Disney, and they had their cultural attachés shipping those movies back home all the time. Then, too, she was always fond of American songs, either music from the mass or American popular songs. Her favorite was "Tea for Two" which she had translated into German. In the bunker during the final days when all these people were so frantic and trying to cut each other's throat and Hitler's throat and trying to escape somehow, she seemed to be quite serene and happy there singing "Tea for Two" quite a lot.

But, still, she's a puzzle to me. You know, loyalty is so hard to find, and so valuable. She was loyal when everybody else was being disloyal. At the same time, you have to ask—loyalty to what? She sees that their whole population is being wiped out, that a whole generation of young men is being killed. She worries about that. Yet, she broke up with her sister because her sister said, "He's a demon; he's going to haul the whole country into the abyss!" And this was the sister who had really raised her and whom she had always been terribly close to, and sent her away and wouldn't see her again.

BT: Was it love or was it worship?

WDS: That's a good question. It may be, you know, in some cases there may not be a difference. I don't know. I said that's what interests me, that she's a puzzle to me. I can't help respecting loyalty and at the same time you've got to say loyalty to what? In some sense, to be a Nazi was to be disloyal to the country. The army, for example, took an oath, not to the nation, not to the country, not to the folk, but to HIM! That's a terrible betrayal! And only one single officer had nerve enough to refuse and resign his commission.

BT: One person that I interviewed, that I talked to about the book, said that what you're trying to do here is put faces on these monsters.

WDS: That would suit me alright. They are monsters, but they're human monsters, and I think we all have those capabilities.

BT: Do you think it could happen again in today's world?

WDS: Do you want to pick up the paper? What do you want to look at, Bosnia? There are at least six places in the world right now where there's ethnic cleansing going on. Look at the Tutsis and the Hutus. What were our tax dollars doing in Chile how many years ago?

BT: Could you not get the same point across by maybe focusing on more of the atrocities rather than on the people that perpetrated them? For example, could you have conveyed that same idea by writing a book about the Holocaust?

WDS: I don't think so. I am in no way opposed to writing such a book. There are a great many. I've read a great many of them. That serves a purpose. It also has a certain amount of danger involved in it; you're identifying there with the victim, and I think that's a very dangerous thing. For instance, the Nazis saw themselves as victims of World War I and of the treaty at the Hall of Versailles, the Hall of Mirrors. Seeing yourself as a victim can be very dangerous. That doesn't necessarily follow, but it seems to me if you don't see that you also have the capability of being a victimizer, then you're skipping half of the most important part of the evidence. The point is: the chances are if somebody is victimizing you, you can't control that. But you can, at least, control yourself from becoming a victimizer.

BT: So there is some value for you in kind of looking at this from the other side?

WDS: Oh, yes, certainly. I've done all that. I've read it all. I get weary, I confess, of reading things, all those men Solzhenitsyn writes about; I believe those men are awful, I believe they're rotten. I don't need to wallow too much in the bloody details of it. I know something about what that's like, and it can clearly get to be a kind of fixation and a dangerous one in which you see yourself as good and the other people as wicked. I think I started writing these poems with the same feeling that everybody had; how could those people have done those things? And then more and more you look at the history of your own people, and your history since World War II, and you begin to see something about, yes, that's how they could have done those things.

BT: Did you make that shift?

WDS: I think gradually. I mean as I look back at it, it seems to me that that's how my feeling about it has changed very slowly over many, many years.

BT: Did you ever feel like a voyeur? I mean, when you were doing your research and looking at the photographs of dead Nazis. Was there an element of voyeurism in it?

WDS: I suppose so. I haven't worried about it or thought about it, but perhaps—I wouldn't deny it. I have certainly indulged in worse voyeurisms which I will not talk about!

BT: Would you call this book uplifting at all?

WDS: Ummmm. I don't even know what's meant by uplifting. It's a term I don't use.

BT: Do you think there's hope in this book?

WDS: Some of the people seem rather hopeful to me. For instance, Traudl Junge. She's an interesting person. By the way, her name was Gertrude Humps and she married one of Hitler's adjutants, a man named Hans Junge. At a certain point, Junge became kind of discontented with what they were being told and thought, I guess, "I'm getting everything directly from Hitler. I want to go find out for myself and ask to be transferred to active duty." He did and he was killed. But before he was killed he came back once, and he was so changed, so shaken, that his wife didn't understand it. She just knew that what this man had seen had completely changed him and shaken him right to his boots.

Traudl Junge went on working for Hitler. She was one of the youngest of the secretaries, very popular with Hitler because she was very pretty. But she never believed Hitler again. Sometimes she sort of backslid a little bit as people would put pressure on her to say something in favor of the Nazis, but in general she was already asking why has my parents' house been destroyed, why has my beautiful young husband been killed, why have all these young men, so handsome, so attractive, why are they dead? What's the cause of this. And now she pretty well knew the cause of this, at least the immediate cause. And never fell for Hitler's line again.

She took his last testament; it was just hours before he committed suicide, and she thought, now he will say what it all really is about, what caused it. But she was so disillusioned because she said it was just the same old lies all over again. For instance, he was blaming the Jews for starting the war, whereas at lunch he had said to her again and again, "I wish I had started it sooner." In the last section of the book there's a poem ["Traudl Junge: 'everybody left feels free . . .'"] where she's free to go, Hitler's dead, but to what, and to where, and what's she to believe in, and what's she supposed to do. She's asking.

BT: One final question, perhaps. Do you think you're a better person for having written this book?

WD: You'll have to ask somebody else. I can't judge me. You know, I always think I'm one of the sweetest and most intelligent and kindly of humans. Other people may have a different notion about this, and you'd probably better ask them.

W.D . Snodgrass's *The Fuehrer Bunker:* Ordinary Evil, Extraordinary Knowing

DEVON MILLER-DUGGAN

Most poetry about the period of the Third Reich concentrates its gaze on the Reich's victims, its resistors, and the horror and grief Hitler's reign engendered. W. D. Snodgrass's cycle, *The Fuehrer Bunker*, stares instead at the horror's manufacturers, listening to the workings and squirmings of the minds of Hitler's inner circle as they contemplate the end of their dream, taking the reader on a tour of one of the more fetid sewers of the twentieth-century mind—a sucking morass of what might be the worst case of *mentalité* in Western history. Snodgrass had hoped, in fact, to be able to use an x-ray of Hitler's brain on the cover of the book,[1] implying that the bunker and its occupants were products of Hitler's brain, that all the poems spoken in the book are products of his mind, that the bunker was Hitler's brain, or that Hitler's brain was the bunker.

Reviewers have tended not to know what to make of such an extraordinary project, and *The Fuehrer Bunker* has been called everything from an extraordinarily unpleasant artistic success to an anti-Semitic tract. That the poems wade through the mire of the Nazi psyche with wit, elegance, and technical brilliance is what makes them both important and bewildering. No technique appears here except in the service of the poems' intention: form and wit confess in these poems as much as the words the characters speak, but they also amuse and beguile.

While the soliloquies are unpleasant and every bit as shocking as they were intended to be, they are not irresponsible. Based on extensive research, they stay very close to the facts, neither sympathizing nor excusing. The monologues from the *Bunker*, exploring as they do the banality and commonality of evil as components of the human makeup, may be a kind of ultimate poetry of witness and confession. When in preparation for writing, Snodgrass interviewed Albert Speer, he asked what Speer thought had gone wrong in the Reich. Speer answered that Hitler had "neglected his knowing," a phrase Snodgrass later used in Speer's soliloquies. All great journeys into the underworld involve the acquisition of knowledge, and the comparison between Snodgrass's journey into Hitler's bunker and Dante's tour of hell has already been made by Donald Hall in a jacket blurb for an earlier edition. Where Dante's guide was Virgil, Snodgrass's silent guide is Sigmund Freud. In an intricate transference Snodgrass takes on the "I" of Adolf Hitler and Magda Goebbels, using the dramatic monologue to make confessions darker and more general than anything by other confessional poets.

The cycle observes a variety of obsessions, degradations, and evils—Hitler's kinks, Josef Goebbels's sexual gluttony, Magda Goebbels's infanticides. Just as writing each voice forces Snodgrass to inhabit each of the I's he writes, his reader also inhabits that I, speaking along with both poet and character. The reader has other roles as well—listener, confessor, spy, analyst, possible jury, helpless judge—both I and eye—all facets of the reader's role as knower.

The title page of *The Fuehrer Bunker* features epigraphs from two of the unlikeliest sources ever to have been paired on a title page. The first is from a late remark by Goebbels: "Even if we lose this war, we still win, for our spirit will have penetrated our enemies' hearts." The second cites Mother Teresa's reply to the question of when she began her mission: "On the day I discovered I had a Hitler inside me." The epigraphs state the philosophical boundaries the poem inhabits and are a hedge against misinterpretation of the poem as reveling in its characters. As a confession for all of us, ritualized by its formal structures, *The Fuehrer Bunker* is possibly presumptuous. But it is hardly a presumption based on flimsy evidence. If the poems are a confession from Snodgrass about Snodgrass, it is the same confession Mother Teresa makes. It means that he will not ask the reader to make any confessions he has not been willing to make. The epigraphs do not explain our confession; they make it impossible for us to deny confessing: Hitler is in us. A monster of rhetoric tells us and a saint acknowledges it.

If knowing (and not knowing) is the cycle's theme, time and character are the poem's physical structures. Each of the sections is dated and follows approximately the historical chronology. Each of the poems is also dated—like dispatches from hell. The dominant structure is, however, character. Each of the speakers has a formally distinct voice. No one speaks or writes every day. The secretary Traudl Junge and the Goebbels's daughter, Helga, each speak once. After Old Lady Barkeep's seventeen poems, the voices of Goebbels and Heinrich Himmler dominate the sequence with eleven and ten poems respectively. Magda and Herman Goering both have seven poems. Hitler speaks five, Speer six. Three military commanders speak—Gotthard Heinrici has four poems, Helmuth Weidling three, Hermann Fegelein one. Every character speaks, consciously or unconsciously, about the issue of what he or she knows, wishes to know, longs to have known, doesn't want to know, is trying not to know, thinks others know, wants others to know, hopes knowing will do, hopes not knowing will do, is afraid to know, refuses to know—every conceivable shade of relationship between the knower and the known.

The cycle's focus on the functionaries—some cynical, some obsessed, some repulsive, and some just trying to get out of the war with their skins and some portion of Germany intact—suggests that all the bunker's inhabitants are parts of Hitler, severed and barricaded from each other, making Hitler an ultimate instance of the shattered subject. By choosing to write in the voices of the complicitous as well as the active, Snodgrass eliminates the problem of preaching. Including voices ranging from Hitler's to his secretary's and the Goebbels's children's, he writes the voice of EveryGerman, or every human, and so speaks from within the congregation—from the pit, not from the pulpit.

The cycle opens with a character from the pit. She is Old Lady Barkeep, Snodgrass's version of a figure "Berliners revived . . . from Renaissance song and verse, Frau Wirtin, [and used as the source of] . . . satirical verses . . . about their leaders." An unnamed chorus of Berliners sings Old Lady Barkeep's songs. Her introductory analysis of the war's progress is accurate and succinct:

Old Lady Barkeep had a Folk
Who got their gun when Hitler spoke;
    He bellowed, "Germany, waken!
Rise up; if any foe rejects us,
We'll broil their liver for our breakfast
    And fry their balls like bacon!

"If they bite back, the bloody cunts,
We'll bang them on two fronts at once;
    You can't resist a God!"
Like ladykillers at a dance,
His troops advanced in goosestep prance
Through Austria, Czechoslovakia, France,
    Then found they'd shot their wad.

Easter in 1945
Was April Fools' Day. The one drive
They could maintain was to survive.
    Through caves and cellar holes,
Ditches and subway tunnels then
These irresistible Supermen
    Crept like ants or moles.

The elastic stanza, reminiscent of the limerick, bounces along, coming down at the end of each stanza on some important point. And because of its resemblance to the limerick, the stanza casts all of its information in the form of dirty jokes, so that no matter how brutal the narrative is, the narrator shrugs and smirks knowingly. The vehemence of frying the enemy's liver for breakfast—the kind of primitive warrior behavior the Nazi myth lionized—is insufficiently violent; the enemy's genitals must also be eaten. It is an ironic consumption suggesting that German troops needed more than their own testicles. The next, more virulently sexual, stanza finds the troops, having engaged in double gang rape at the behest of a Zeus-Hitler, are in fact short of semen. They can no longer fuck Europe, so they hide, or the leaders hide, like moles or ants. Rape is a perverse kind of burrowing-into. Both moles and ants muck up the surface as they burrow. Both are also functionally blind—precisely the problem the bunker's denizens suffer from. They will not see, and will not know the things Old Lady Barkeep not only knows, but sings.

The final stanza introduces the first of the monologuists, Minister of Propaganda Joseph Goebbels, whose job it is to see to it that no one sees. Old Lady Barkeep quotes him telling the truth, if inadvertently: "'if it costs all your lives, my dears, / Our reign will last a thousand years! / Or twelve—same price." The "dears" he addresses could be the people of Berlin or his family. Both Old Lady Barkeep and Goebbels are verbally facile, ferociously vulgar, and not particularly moral (she only cares about the stupidity and waste of Hitler's war). But where she says "shit" when she smells it, Goebbels takes a deep breath and tells everyone else they're smelling flowers.

Dr. Joseph Goebbels, clubfoot, womanizer, and father of six children named in honor of the Fuehrer, speaks almost invariably in rhymed couplets or triplets, the most obviously mnemonic of all rhyme schemes.[2] Nearly all of his poems contain more than one voice, emphasizing his essential inability to speak out of one side of his mouth. He weaves bits of old songs, foul limericks, children's prayers, and his nasty commentary on his propaganda into all but two of his poems. The first of his single-voiced poems is spoken on the day he moves into the lowest level of the bunker, the second as he and his wife Magda go upstairs into the garden where they commit suicide.

Goebbels, who had tried to make careers as a socialist polemicist, a priest, and a novelist before he found the Nazi party, was a classically unquiet soul—a partially crippled man in the hierarchy of a government that institutionalized the worship of physical perfection. Like Hitler, he was small and dark, but preached the Aryan religion of blondness and size. He was among the century's most deft practitioners of doublespeak, yet he behaved, at the end of the war, with absolute clarity. He has many of the traits of a religious convert. He sees the role of the Reich (1 April) as nothing less than the salvation of humankind, and all of Hitler's decisions as redemptive and mystical:

> So once more, the Chief's wrong proves out
> Better than my right. I, no doubt,
> Could have curbed slaughter, ruin, terror—
> Just my old sentimental error.
> Our role is to wipe out a twisted
> Life that should never have existed.

At the end of the same poem, Goebbels blesses him "who dares act out his worst . . ." and then prays:

> Our Father who art in Nihil,
> We thank Thee for this day of trial
> And for the loss that teaches self-denial.
> Amen.

Later, Goebbels will quote Carlyle and Goethe to himself, reassure himself that he "knew which of my lies were lies"; narrate his life story while looking at old photographs of his unprepossessing child-self; contemplate selling his services to the Russians; interlineate his speech for Hitler's final birthday with a commentary contemptuous of both his Chief and his Chief's loyal subjects; review his opinions of the rest of Hitler's nearest; quote *The Nibelungenlied*, the other great German myth, and explain his lusts and his life by saying that he "loved only the holes in things." This Goebbels loves Hitler at the same time that he professes himself incapable of love. He loves having something to love, and hates himself for his need, hating the object of his love for accepting him. Even dazzled by living in the bunker with Hitler, he knows himself for Hitler's intellectual pimp, but sees himself as a chaos in search of external control, and mistakes that insight for wisdom. Although he keeps looking, Goebbels is unwilling to re-form himself for yet another master, partially from fear of the Russians, but also because Nazism has become his Truth. He cannot cut himself free, even though he tries, in his last-birthday speech for Hitler, to sever himself from words: "Henceforth, I never will speak word." He also refers to himself as both Pan and Vulcan, concerned always to write himself into myth, and never satisfied with just one.

He succeeds, finally. In his last poem (1 May), Goebbels directs himself through his suicide. He fusses with his appearance and reminds himself to act with dignity as he moves on to "infect history." "The rest," he says, "is silence. Left like sperm / In a stranger's gut, waiting its term." History is now a strange woman he can rape and impregnate—an inverted theology of the Incarnation—and he and Magda, going into a garden to die, have become an inverted Adam and Eve, damned by eating from the tree of half-knowledge.

Himmler, according to Old Lady Barkeep, is another repeated failure who blossomed in the compost pile of National Socialism. He wants to see his role as leader of the SS as "similar / To being Christ or Pope." But he is only a detail-man, a member of a class notorious for its inability to see the Big Picture and its tendency to overrate its own importance. Part of the problem is Himmler's reliance on systems; he believes ardently in astrology, eugenics, spying, and measurements.

Printed on graph paper, Himmler's poems consist entirely of capital letters. Periods separate each of the words. Each line consists of precisely thirty characters, and each stanza has five unrhymed lines and is an alphabet acrostic. The poems consist of five-stanza groups, each containing five or ten stanzas. The obsessive formality of Himmler's poems throws into high relief the insanity of their content. It is almost possible to see his tense grip on a pen poised over paper squared-off like the map of a battlefield. Graph paper is used by designers and mathematicians to help them make exact graphs or keep scale. Himmler's scale is wholly off, his designs unbalanced, his overview skewed, his knowledge warped. Ironically, he may be the cycle's most accurate speaker: his fussy, pseudoorderly, pseudoscientific, pseudostrategic ramblings illustrate precisely the institution and workings of National Socialism—perfect phalanxes of perfect disorder.

Speaking of a group of *Lebensborn*[3] children (15 April) who have accidentally fetched up in army headquarters south of Berlin, Himmler says they are the flowers in "THE. HUMAN.GARDEN" out of which Jews and gypsies must be weeded:

> VALUABLE.BIG.BLOND.&.BLUE-EYED
> WHEN.YOU.HELD.INSPECTION.THERE
> YOU.ALWAYS.FOUND.THEM.FRESH.AS
> ZINNIAS.IN.A.WELL-SELECTED.BED.

Himmler extends the metaphor about the "weeding out" of lesser races into his private ramblings, revealing its essential silliness at the same time that "SELECTED" recalls the selections at Auschwitz. At the end of the poem, Himmler worries about these children reverting to old feelings and turning on their Nazi trainers, concluding that "WE.MUST.RUSH.THEM.OUT.OF. / ZOS-

SEN.OR.'DISINFECT'.THEM.NOW." In previous poems he had
been desperately reading the stars. In his next poem he discusses
again the necessity of weeding out even Germany's perfect flowers, but then returns to worrying about himself, fretting for
twenty-five lines over the most face-saving, sympathy-producing
way to greet Eisenhower, concentrating on surfaces. His poem
dated 20 April continues in this vein, fretting about his good
name, how many decisions he thinks he's being asked to make,
what to do with the remaining Jews, and Hitler's obvious mad-
ness. The poem's last line simply wonders, cartoon fashion,
"OH.WHAT.TO.DO.TO.DO.TO.DO."

Himmler spends the next few poems in the same dither, worrying about his moral duty to keep his wife in luxury, his bor-
rowing from Bormann of party funds and subsequent
vulnerability, and most of all about his chances of succeeding
Hitler and continuing the Reich's work of making an orderly
Germany. He even sees himself (23 April) stuck between bowel
movements: "ALWAYS.THE.SAME.DILEMMAS.STUCK / BE-
TWEEN.STOOLS. BALANCING . . ." His graph-paper precision
and obsessive collection of data separate him from knowledge
rather than keeping him orderly and informed. His is the most
graphic metaphor for the utter failure of the Reich's systems to
keep its functionaries mindful. The people in Snodgrass's bunker
have replaced thinking with systems, suggesting that systems are
where the hitlers thrive.

Unlike Himmler, Reichsmarshall Hermann Goering tells himself a certain amount of truth and listens to it, torturing himself.
His first six poems are made up of questions—riddles, an imagined inquisition by accountants, three versions of a pre-
interrogation questionnaire, a riddling interrogation, Goering's
own grilling of his wardrobe, and an imagined SS interrogation—
but because all the questions occur in the mind-bunker of his
self-absorption, nothing comes of them. His final poem, spoken
as he stands naked in front of a mirror awaiting an actual SS
interrogation, acknowledges the uselessness of his knowing:
"You might as well find out just what you've done, / Though
that's not what they'll hang you for." Except for the questionnaire
and his final poem, Goering's poems consist of six-line stanzas
with an *abccba* rhyme scheme which turns on itself as he turns
on himself (1 April):

You led our Flying Circus; how
Could our war ace become a clown?
Both pad out extended fronts;
Both make their living from slick stunts;
All the same, both get shot down.
But only one's called Meier now.[4]

The questionnaire from 16 April, the middle of the cycle, is
Goering's turning point. Its formal structures, repeated three
times with three different sets of answers, push him beyond easy
answers. The document includes three headings for his name—
"NAME OF THE PRISONER," "PRISONER'S CORRECT NAME,"
and "PRISONER IS CALLED"—position, address, bloodlines,
aliases, hobbies, feats, war crimes, and "FATE". His fate changes
from "Successor to the Chief" to "A swift death on the field"
and then to "The lime pit or the rope." He uses a different name
each time he identifies himself, beginning with his reportedly
Jewish stepfather's surname, "Hermann von Epenstein," moving
on to his legal name, then to his nickname, "Herr Reaktion,"
accurate since in his politics he reacts rather than acts. In a
separate category of "IDENTITY," he names himself "Herr Meier,
the homeless Jew." Under the last name he tells the truth: he
neglects his father, consorts with "Men of bad conscience," uses
drugs, tells jokes while bombs fall "outside." He also admits that
his "cities lie in ruins" and that he "supplied / [His] men no
rations, no ammunition, and no hope."

In his last poem his six-line stanza gives way to a nine-line
stanza with a stuttering *abaccbdcd* rhyme scheme. The longer
stanza form matches the breakdown of his thinking—the Sene-
can dictum about time and brevity brought to life: Goering is
running out of time, so his words overrun his form. Again, Snodgrass makes the form of the poem mimic and comment on the
poem's speaker. Goering's frightful insecurity clings to the orna-
ment of rhyme even when he stands in front of a mirror naked,
and his childish self-absorption expends all its energy imagining
people paying attention to him, questioning him, looking to him
for answers. If we think that asking questions is a sufficient road
to knowledge, then Snodgrass's Goering proves us wrong.

Albert Speer's poems dissolve their own form as the cycle
progresses, looking more and more like Hitler's. Old Lady Bar-

keep introduces him blandly, referring to him as her architect and *her* builder, commenting only that he made "clever / Illusions in the skies but never / Brought light to their price." His early poems consist of right-triangle stanzas in unrhymed, mirror-imaged pairs looking like architectural ornaments Speer might have designed. The stanzas play with the image of a pair of buildings, one above and the other burrowing into the earth, with one upright (short-to-long lines) and the other running, not upside-down, but back down (long-to-short), the lines broken purely for spacing. Where Himmler's poems conform to a compulsion for emphasis and order, Speer's reveal a fixation with a single size and design reflecting the uniform "design" of life under the Reich. The upright stanzas, in bold type, contain Speer's narration of Hitler's orders and his efforts to subvert them. The bold type makes the voice loud—a voice for public record. He questions his actions and motivations and Hitler's intentions in the inverted stanzas, in normal type. But the triangles always reverse, repeating the tunneling in and out of information and justification, eventually breaking down or blending the two typefaces, so that Speer's struggle to contain what he knows and doesn't want to know in orderly constructs turns itself to rubble.

Even in the poem in which Speer speaks of his decision to subvert Hitler's scorched earth policy (20 April), the knowledge of other horrors invades his attempt to envision himself as part of an amoral structure in which he can compensate for Hitler:

> What was it
> Hanke saw there in the East?
> And warned me not
> to find out, not to see? What
> are the Russians digging up?
> the sort of things
> I saw in the camps—
> forced labor, wretched conditions . . .

What the Russians are *digging up* is not conditions but bodies by the thousands. Even as he allows some real knowledge to break into his carefully arranged knowing, thereby shattering the formal patterns of his poems, Speer turns away from it and back to his carefully pyramidal stanza. But the break is irreparable, and in the poem's final stanza, although its shape is perfect, the bold and normal-types mix, and a third typeface enters:

He forbids us all to smoke
then sends us all up the chimney.
(*What chimney? Where?*) **Idiot, use your**
eyes. If he has his way we won't have one
chimney standing. And does he neglect his knowing
I did not and I will not obey him? He may well know I
am going out to betray him. **Too certainly, he knows that I**
am faithful. **Knows that I** evade my better self. **Knows that I**
neglect my knowing. That he and I, together, we **neglect our knowing.**

Speer knows what he doesn't know, that he chooses not to know, that knowledge breaks the shell of his form. Not only do Speer's voices become muddled, his distance from Hitler, or ability to distinguish himself from Hitler, becomes frail. Three of the lines end in "I", and the pronoun appears six times in four lines, revealing Speer's attempt to cling to his own personality while he watches Hitler's dissolve. Three days later in the cycle, his pyramids return, but crumble again, sometimes disappearing, sometimes shrinking, as he wonders why they all let Hitler live and how they can manage not to know about Auschwitz:

    No.
    No man
    Ever knows
    About such things.
    We know only how much
    Each person knows he knows . . .
        We must keep faith with that
    Until the Russians come . . .

In his next poem, the bold-face voice disappears altogether and the smaller pyramid-stanzas blend with short, unevenly margined stanzas, couplets, and gothic-type quotations from Faust. He reviews the history of the Reich and regrets the destruction of all he has built and planned. In history as well as in the cycle, Speer is the first of the major figures to leave the bunker, he disappears after 24 April. In his final lines, the pyramids are gone, Faust is gone, he knows that he will build nothing more grandiose than "[t]in shacks to get this week's survivors / through next winter."

Hitler's mistress follows Hitler's architect in the cycle. Old Lady Barkeep introduces Braun as a gift from her, the German Everywoman, to Hitler to "comfort [him] in his distress" and comments bitterly that, having been given this gift/toy/houri by the German people, he then proceeded to keep his relationship with her a secret:

> But for prestigious, high-style wooin',
> Disclosure to the public's viewin',
> Even old-fashioned bill and cooin',
>   Or just plain screwin',
>   Nothin' doin'.

Appropriately enough for someone risen from the people, Braun is blissfully obsessed with how far she has risen and how indelibly she has made her mark on history. She knows that she has beaten out the other women in Hitler's life to finally become his wife. Beyond her life with Hitler, she exhibits little consciousness of anything else except the crowds who have always stolen his time, and occasionally her mother, who has not approved of her unmarried state. Her first poem consists of five-line stanzas in simple *ababa* rhyme, interlaced with lines from an American popular song. In her second poem, after air raids have forced her into the bunker, the stanza length varies between four and six lines, the rhyme is gone, and the song has been replaced by bits from a requiem mass. Her unrhymed third poem, spoken ecstatically after she decides to stay with Hitler and die, features snatches from "Tea For Two," which the epigraph says she liked to sing to irritate Hitler. Its stanzas range between five and eight lines. On 25 April, while she chooses snapshots to complete her photo album, an interviewer's voice invades her six-line stanzas, but the orderly alternating rhyme (*ababab*) has returned. At this point, running through her poem and her head is a popular German love song about giving all for love. In her final delirious poem margins, rhyme, and regular stanzas all disappear into the mix of her history with Hitler, the mass, the marriage ceremony, and self-congratulation. Her poems' formal structures do not so much break down as go up in flames.

Braun cannot even see herself except in photographs, which she spends two of her five poems looking at. Even staring at her own photos, and imagining herself in a postmortem conversation about them with an unnamed "researcher," she cannot entirely believe her own existence, and speaks of herself in the third person (1 April):

> Can films lie? Not these. She saved
> these candid snapshots as a true
> image, brought back to life, preserved,
> a joyful life that no one knew,
> of a great love no one believed.
>
> **I can't believe**
> **That you believe in me.**

While some of this disbelief is coy posturing, some of it is also a function of a disordered personality. Further, the fictional Braun's questioning of her own existence illustrates the whole cycle's intricate relationship between historical fact and poet's fiction: in a cycle based on historical documents, a character who is a blend of fact and imagination questions her existence. That she offers photographs as evidence of her existence is particularly ironic, given the role of photographs in proving Nazi crimes. That she uses American popular songs, made-up romances the historical Braun loved, to question herself only heightens the ironies. She does not even have her own words.

In her final poem, where she speaks of her last-act marriage to Hitler, Braun's voice changes from her earlier chirp and snicker, becoming sometimes biblical, and sometimes coldly self-aware:

> Now each one has the nothing
> they fought for. My mother—
> she only wants it all
> to mean her meaning; something
> instead of life. To tell the neighbors.
> And that I give her. She
> can rest.
>
> ....
>
> My mother's will be mine.
> Is mine.

When in her last line she, not Hitler or Christ, speaks Christ's words, "it is accomplished," does she see herself, not her Fuehrer, as martyr to the cause of the Reich? Snodgrass leaves her on the edge of her purdah, bound in a mess of religion and delusion. It is one of Snodgrass's ironies that this almost-knowing should bloom in the slightest of the main characters in the cycle, teasing the reader just as Braun herself has spent her adult life teasing Hitler with sex and suicide.

The final poem in the opening section is Hitler's. Formally, Hitler's poems are the most chaotic of the poems in the *Bunker*. They are among the longest as well—rambling, polyvocal digressions into the past, present, and future, metaphorical clouds of pathological unknowing. Even more so than Goebbels's poems, Hitler's are punctuated by stage directions, as though the Fuehrer were a play. Hitler's poems share with those of Goebbels's and Speer's a tendency to break into passages from great works of German literature, which appear in traditional gothic typeface. Hitler's first words, spoken on I April, are "Down: I got it all. Almost." As he speaks them, he sits in a room in the bunker's lowest level, like Satan at the bottom of Dante's hell, reading battle reports in front of a wall map. The "it" he has almost gotten is, first of all, Europe, but is also the truth about the tide of the war since Stalingrad, and about his dreams of an invincible Germany and a Jew-free Europe. The "it" is also a cake his mother baked for his brother that Hitler ate most of, as well as his mother's love. His poems touch all of these elements, as well as sex, disloyalty, the cowardice of any German who doesn't want to die, hatred for the Jew-loving Americans, his murdered niece Geli, and his failing commanders. He speaks one nine-line stanza in a later poem, but can generally maintain his concentration on any topic for no more than six lines, most often no more than three, after which he shifts and quotes himself, his generals, Wagner's *Lohengrin*, Disney films, *Die Goetterdaemerung*, his biographers, or his detractors. His dominant voices normally speak in pentameter, but there is literally neither regular rhyme nor reason in these poems. Snodgrass's Hitler is more rabid than mad-venomous, unable to swallow (the truth, in this case), driven to destroy as much as possible before he finally dies. But he will, in his five poems, confess nearly everything. He will not, however, seek absolution. This Hitler prefers to wallow in self-justification and blame everyone else in his life for the failure of his dream. He calls himself a "Brat fed sick on sugartits," referring to his having been nursed too long, and to having been grossly over-indulged by his mother, then turns wistful: "Truly, you regret how kind you've been."

In the midst of his kindness, he refers to his own soldiers on April 1 as "gutless," the Berliners as "ditchworms," and his enemies as "trash rats." His language is vivid and compelling, but also crude and cruel. He cannot tolerate anything alive or seeking life, referring to the buds on the trees in Berlin's bombed-out spring as "[t]hat sickly green scum, filming the trees again." His animadversions on everything that shows signs of not dying are broken into by his meditations on his power ("So shall I swallow all this ground / Till we two shall be one flesh."), his potency as a speaker ("From ten million speakers / My voice scattering like farmers' rain."), and his increasing weakness ("Since Stalingrad, / This shuddering I can't control."). The last voice, like the first, refers to cake, with Hitler asking whiningly, "We could still find a little chocolate cake? / A teensy bit of schlag, perhaps?" on the heels of another of his voices praising Stalin's rapaciousness: "belts, bones, Buckles—nothing sticks in that man's craw."

The first of five sets of margins, roughly fifteen spaces to the right, contains stage directions—"(takes a situation report)". This is also the margin in which Hitler gloats about his relationship with his mother, and the margin in which he recalls a time when Hindenberg praised his "swift gallantry" and men he sent to firing squads "heiled [his] name." This voice functions as an elegy for the halcyon days of Hitler's ascendancy. The second margin, further to the left of the first, indicating a more prominent voice, is the most recurrent voice in the poem—the bile-spewing, ranting voice of the defeated conqueror. The third margin, five spaces to the right of the first, indicates a nearly reflective discourse. In it, Hitler questions and dismisses the costs of his rise and reign: "'Casualties? But that is what / The young men are there for'." It is also the voice in which he notes his own physical disintegration.

He uses another margin to speak in more complex terms of his mother and of the consequences of her spoiling. He sees "[h]er

open grave's mouth, speaking." The next stanza in which this
voice/margin speaks also uses imagery of oral consumption. Hitler says, referring to both his mother's grave and his field map,
that "this ground would devour me. / So shall I swallow all this
ground / Till we two shall be one flesh." He uses both the language of eating and of the marriage rite. It is not clear that he
knows the distinction between marrying his mother and
marrying Europe, between consuming and marrying, or between
living and dying, since earth is the "one flesh" into which living
things disappear. The voice speaks as if it were a Miltonic fallen
angel: "The evils I do not desire, I do and I survive."

Hitler's second poem, although polyvocal like the first, is a
sustained gloat barely punctuated with one-line reminders of the
might of the Russian army pressing in on Berlin. All of the voices
in his head sing songs to him of his own omnipotence and his
omnivorousness. The murder/death of his niece and lover Geli
Raubal figures prominently in the litany of triumph. In his birthday poem from 20 April, a voice not his observes someone who
may or may not be Hitler engaged in coprophilia.[5] The poem
begins like most of the poems, with a stage-setting epigraph:

> (After his birthday ceremony, Hitler with-
> draws to his sitting room where he holds one
> of Blondi's puppies. Lines from Lohengrin
> surface in his thoughts).

The poem's first lines, "Best stuffed in a bag and drowned. / This
mockery: my best bitch / Pregnant once she can't survive," are
so brutal that it makes us wonder whether the "bitch" to be
drowned is Blondi or Braun. The next line, bumped five spaces
into the left margin, begins the description of the defecation-
ritual: "The man will lie on his back; he is, of course, completely
naked." These are the longest lines in Hitler's poems, drawing
themselves out, teasing the reader by breaking the act into tiny
units, interspersing them with rants and recollections. The voice
intends to be scientific—precise, commentating, and explana-
tory: "it is not the mere fact of the urine or faeces that matters. /
Rather, he must be able to watch as these emerge into existence."
The "of course" and "mere" are typical of the voice, subtle comments indicating a certain scholarly relish on the part of the

teller, who tells the story to instruct or illustrate, but enjoys the slight naughtiness, the shock value of the rare perversion. One of the more telling clues to the identity of the voice is the use of the Latinate spelling *faeces*. If Freud has been Snodgrass's Virgil, then this may be the place in the cycle where the reader actually hears him speak, either directly or through a disciples's voice.

The remaining material in the poem—more memories of Hitler's obsessive mother, further ranting, bits of his philosophy ("A man who would accept / What is, is criminal, too vile to live."), and exclamations from *Lohengrin*—constitutes another opening of the bowels of Hitler's mind. There is even a moment of relative truth-telling:

> My pills; Morrell's injections.
> My cake, chairs, rugs—without them,
> Bare concrete. Same as any
> Jew degenerate at Auschwitz.

The whole resembles, somewhat, the ramble and revelation of the therapeutic process, with Hitler as analysand.[6] As is the case with so much that issues from the mind's depths, the revelation of Hitler's peculiarly repulsive proclivities is both trivial and significant. Although not information we are particularly happy to have, it points out an essential uselessness of information: knowing Hitler's perversion helps us understand nothing, except that this man does not like life. Psychology turns out to be another failed religion, another failed system. The gossip does, however, reconfigure the bunker as the *anus mundi*, not Auschwitz. The digested, rejected, and a-nutritive materials of the Western psyche wash down the hole of the bunker, and Hitler sits at the bottom, ecstatically, incoherently receiving it, calling for more.

Oral and eating imagery fill Hitler's penultimate poem (28 April), in which he muses over the hanging death of Mussolini. He calls Mussolini the "flesh that died for me," punning grossly on Communion. Hitler accuses the people of Europe, Mussolini's murderers, of wanting to "[f]lush me out like an enema, / Like douching after sex." In a pun that manages to be both scatological and eschatological, he declares that he wants "only one thing: the end! the end!".

   Hitler's final poem on April 30, spoken after Braun's suicide and before his own, continues the spew, roiling from discussion to discussion and voice to voice across five margins. In these last utterances, he quotes himself or words Goebbels has written for him, counts and re-counts his murders, fumes about betrayal and the venality of his followers, quotes from various odd sources, misquotes Christ, stares at and dismisses Braun's body, and asserts, as he bites his capsule, that he is

> Winning,
>> winning,
>>> winning.

Even when dying, he sounds like a two-year old having a tantrum. Europe has proven to be too much for him to swallow. That failure has also been too much for him to swallow. The only thing he can swallow is death, the only thing at the beginning and at the end that he has ever been willing to know.

   The last of the major characters to speak, Magda Goebbels speaks the most formally traditional and varied poems in the cycle—a pantoum, a variation on the ballade, a series of linked villanelles, another series of linked triolets, an extended villanelle, and nursery rhyme stanzas. In the end, after she has murdered her children, she speaks in a stanza form whose pattern is derived from the card game Solitaire, which she plays while drinking champagne and waiting for her own death. All of her poems are spoken in drearily regular iambs, and she addresses herself in the second person, like a ladies' magazine article. She has no set poetic form, having no personality beyond a rabid desire to please Hitler. Her poems use traditional forms because her public persona as the perfect Nazi woman consisted of a hyper-traditional construct of womanhood. Her last poem strays from traditional form because killing one's children is not a traditional norm; by severing her children's lives, she severs her own womanhood, leaving herself solitary. Magda's poems focus on two subjects—the fate of her six children and her obsessive love for Hitler. Her opening pantoum on April 15 considers whether to accept her sister-in-law's offer to get the children behind the American lines. The pantoum repeats the line "To let them live. It might be for the best" and then swallows it up in its next repetition of "Yet our Fuehrer would brand that as flat treason." The pantoum, in which lines two and four of each stanza become lines three and five of the next, is a formal reflection of the endless circling of an argument with oneself, and a formal reflection of a mind unable to process either moral or factual information. That the pantoum itself is a form with no fixed pattern for closure teases the reader with the possibility that Magda's ruminations could take her somewhere new, but Snodgrass ties the pantoum up in the same knot in which Magda ties her thinking. Her second poem is an eight-stanza ballade with an irregular rhyme scheme on nine rhymes in which each stanza begins with the assertion "You can destroy," which also functions as the poem's envoy or conclusion. Again, its formal, repetitive, closed structure mirrors Magda's inability to think her way out of the formal, Hitler-obsessed mold into which she has poured herself. The ballade's structure is even more elaborately knotty than the pantoum's, just as Magda's thinking has become even more tightly bound by her obsessions.

In her next poem (22 April), a series of linked extended villanelles, she begins by asking "How can you do the things you know you'll do?" and asserts that she has "just one desire left: to be true." The villanelle, repeating those two lines five and four times throughout its twenty-two lines, turns them into a rehearsal of her thinking herself into what she'll do, practicing and memorizing her rationale and her fear that she won't live up to her own standards. The next villanelle/strophe begins, "How can you live through what life brings you to?" and goes on to the self-justifying "All of us find it hard just to be true," developing the questions she asks in the first. Her revolving verse forms look at themselves, but she does not. She sees herself as the embodiment of a manufactured identity, the perfect traditional Aryan woman, and speaks in corsetting verse forms that constrict and restrain. After the series of villanelles, her next poem follows an even more restrictive form, the triolet. While the triolet mirrors the extreme discipline she convinces herself to demonstrate, and reinforces the sense of her as a woman caught in false forms, its obsessive repetitions also create a madsong, a lunatic lyric in which the speaker beats her head against the walls of her own mind.

Magda narrates the murders of her six children (30 April) in nursery rhyme cadences recalling "This is the House that Jack Built." One of those murders is of a mentally retarded child (the boy, who may or may not have been Hitler's son), and therefore legal according to Reich law. Magda shoves a spoon with the fluid cyanide between their "tight / Teeth" after Dr. Haase shoots them full of morphine, telling them that "This is the serum that can cure / Weak hearts; these pure, clear drops insure / You'll face what comes and can endure." Having already killed the children, she does not need to comfort them; she needs to comfort herself, reverting to a song-form she might have sung as a child, and might have sung to her children. Never very bright, Magda Goebbels has proved herself the perfect student of the Third Reich, accepting truth only in forms so elaborately decorated that she could stare at them for years and see only the decorations. But she knows one true thing. She knows that her death is what she has become.

Snodgrass has certainly spent much of his poetic life laying out in his poetry his failures as a parent, a husband, and a scholar. But his intention is not to declare his victimhood. His confessions have been of his sins and failures, not his pains or illnesses. If we are to read *The Fuehrer Bunker* in the context of Snodgrass's work in order to find clues to its genesis and meaning, it is in the context of "After Experience" and "Elena Ceauçescu's Bed" that we must read it, poems in which Snodgrass explores the monstrous choices we may all make once we have decided to be alive. Whether we agree with the *Bunker's* implications that we are most of us capable of becoming the banal Goering or obsessed Magda, asking the question is important. The speakers in the bunker are not everyman or everywoman, but they could be, under the wrong circumstances. Their geographical position, in a concrete warren deep underground that is simultaneously coffin and colon, makes them both the buried and rejected contents of the human mind.

Since they confess to us, it is apparently from us that they expect absolution, which implies that we might be absolving, if not ourselves, then our potentials for evil—possibly the most discomfiting of the cycle's seductions. Snodgrass has used his formidable technique to maneuver us not into admitting our guilt—that would veer too close to a sermon—but into looking closely at the company into which we could confess and absolve ourselves. Do we wonder whether, after Auschwitz, the writing of poetry is barbaric? Snodgrass makes elegance confront barbarism. If we believe Marguerite Duras that we will not understand Auschwitz until we see ourselves as guards at a gas chamber door, then we must be grateful to Snodgrass. The bunker is in us.

If, as Wallace Stevens said, poetry is supposed to be read with the nerves, then the poems in *The Fuehrer Bunker* intend to scrape themselves along the reader's nerves like sandpaper. If *The Waste Land* is about both the death of myth and the expense of spirit in a waste of shame, *The Fuehrer Bunker* is about the waste of myth and the degradation of spirit in a waste of shamelessness. The bunker is a wasteland, and just as in Eliot's poem, the voices confess that. But there is no peace at the end of Snodgrass's confessions.

Notes

1. In the end the complexities of obtaining permission to use the x-ray proved too daunting for Snodgrass's publisher. The x-ray on the cover is that of an unnamed derelict admitted to a Rochester, N.Y. hospital.

2. Goebbels's rhyme-scheme also results in some remarkable groupings of end words, texts and commentaries in themselves: burst-worst-thirst-accursed-first and Nihil-trial-selfdenial (1 April), German-sermon-vermin and roar-more-total war (20 April), hollow-follow–swallow (23 April), and must-trust-dust (26 April).

3. Many of the *Lebensborn* were particularly Aryan-appearing children "rescued" from their less than perfectly Nazi parents, often Silesian, and brought back to special schools and camps inside Germany to be raised as the new generation of super-Aryans—a sort of carefully indoctrinated genetic starter set.

4. Goering's men apparently called him "Meier, the Homeless Jew," but only behind his back." Meier is a very common German name, and Goering's reference to it here is as much an indication of his fear of becoming unimportant as his fear of becoming Jewish.

5. Hitler apparently enjoyed having the mostly clothed Braun defecate and urinate on his prone and naked body. Snodgrass notes in the Afterword to the first version of the cycle that reportedly ". . . there is . . . [a] film, recently recovered, which records his sexual perversion; Eva Braun had it secretly filmed, fearing that he might abandon her. What perversion it records has not yet been revealed; however, Otto Strasser and other acquaintances of Hitler's, as well as the American Dr. Langer assert that it was the perversion depicted here."

6. Laurence Goldstein discusses the relationship between the *Bunker* in its first published version, confessional poetry, and both Freud and Erikson in "The Fuehrer Bunker and the New Discourse About Nazism," *The Southern Review* 24,1 (1988): 100–114.

The Morality of History in *The Fuehrer Bunker*

DAVID METZGER

IN 1993, LARRY LEVIS RAISED AN IMPORTANT CONCERN ABOUT *THE Fuehrer Bunker*, worrying that Snodgrass's apparent neutrality in presenting the monologues of the Nazis "will be mistaken for a mimetic fallacy, and for what has been called a 'humanizing' of the Nazis, especially by a careless reader who will miss the irony of his work."[1] I think Snodgrass's poems anticipate such a response not only from a careless reader but also from a careful one. For Snodgrass's starting point is an awareness that Nazis *were* human; they sought a "good" and, in pursuit of that "good," they not only tried to eradicate all opposition but also tried to establish a new understanding of history. Their goal? To control historical forces rather than being determined by them.

Snodgrass does let the Nazis have their say, lets them identify just what kind of history will lead to a future already established by their actions. In the poem of April 26, Snodgrass shows us Goebbels, still unbowed by his own impending doom:

> We Nazis used to say
> The Futures never been in doubt;
> That Past's what we must still work out.
> .   .   .   .
>
> I build that Past others will use
> When they need some lie or excuse
> To do exactly what they choose.

He makes the Nazi concept of history even clearer in one of the epigraphs in the volume: "Even if we lose the war, we still win, for our spirit will have penetrated our enemies' hearts." "Our spirit," manifested in historical precedent, will be ineradicable.

Thus, as Hannah Arendt says in "Ideology and Terror," the Nazis, from this perspective, could treat those labeled "a dying race"—those who would die as planned (as well as those who had died)—as already "dead."[2]

If we find Goebbels's—and Hitler's, Goering's, Himmler's, etc.—view of history repugnant, then we could find, simply enough, that their view of the "good" is not ours, and we may, if we like, feel superior. That feeling can be expanded because, historically, the Nazis failed, and, therefore, in spite of Goebbels's proclamations, so did their view of history. However, for twenty years Snodgrass, under attack for treating the Nazis either neutrally or too sympathetically, has been arguing against that kind of response. In interviews, he has often recalled a man from Philadelphia who, after a poetry reading, accused Snodgrass of glorifying the Nazis. Since the audience was offended and howled him down, Snodgrass did not need to reply, but in years after he has often said he had formed a reply. That reply was "You know you can't blame me for humanizing the Nazis. God did that. They *were* human." And he adds, "If you desire to believe that they were not human, then you are guilty of exactly their worst crime, which is what they tried to do to the Jews, to believe that they were not human."[3] If we assume that Snodgrass tried to avoid that crime in constructing The Fuehrer Bunker, how did he do it? What artistic principles did he bring to bear on that work?

Snodgrass has answered that he brought to the Bunker the same principles he has always brought to his work:

> It seems to me that the aim of a work of art surely is to stretch the reader's psyche, to help him to identify with more people, with more life than he normally does. He is only going to be able to do that if you get him past his beliefs about right and wrong which keep him from seeing what ways in which he is like certain other people. And, of course, he is going to object to that when you do it. Picasso said that all art is an aggression against the reader, or against the observer, the listener, or whatever. In some sense, that certainly is true. It certainly is an act of aggression against the reader's narrow definitions of himself and what he believes and what he thinks—which keep him from seeing an awful lot of things. Naturally, that is one of the things behind the complaint of that man in Philadelphia, who was

so upset at me for writing the poem. But he was accusing me in just exactly the way the Nazis liked to accuse people, without any regard for the justice of the accusation, with only the desire to make himself seem morally superior. If the work of art *doesn't* bring the observer to see more of himself than he was aware of before, what use does it have to exist.[4]

What is it that Snodgrass wants the observer to see about himself through the work of art? We could say, and there is considerable evidence for this, that Snodgrass wants us to recognize, as Mother Teresa does in the second epigraph in the volume, that there is a Hitler inside of all of us. And if not Hitler, maybe a Himmler, a Fegelein, or Eva Braun. But I suggest that Snodgrass, beyond attempting to deconstruct our rigid selves and values, wants us to see that we are fully capable of constructing a personal and human history which will not fall apart because we have a Hitler inside. Larry Levis's concern is a valid one, but it misses Snodgrass's dramatization of a concatenation of "histories" that provide an ethical position from which to choose one or another. We can, *The Fuehrer Bunker* says, endure in a world in which competing histories expand, maybe enrich or degrade, but do not contain all of our human possibilities.

The most obvious "history" Snodgrass provides us is the factual one—the chronological sequence in the *Bunker* that goes from 1 April 1945, to 1 May 1945, and is rooted in the documentary evidence provided by files, memoirs, reports, all that data that Snodgrass collected for thirty years. It is the material most accessible and verifiable. In fact, Snodgrass and Paul Gaston once considered publishing an essay establishing the extremely high degree of factuality in the *Bunker*, but decided that there were numerous other ways that those facts were being confirmed.[5] This "factual" history is the common ground between poet and audience, the one that both can share or contest. For Thomas Keaneally, the author of *Schindler's List*, this arena is the most important one. In the preface to his novel, Keaneally tells us that he has used "the texture and devices of a novel to tell a true story"; in doing this, he has wished "to avoid all fiction, since fiction would debase the record."[6] For Snodgrass, the record is the starting point: he is careful to introduce each poem with a parenthetical expression detailing each poem's particular historical source or moment, but his relationship to the facts is the opposite of Keaneally's: "A true fact," says Snodgrass, "which doesn't feel true in the poem is no good at all. The poem has to feel authentic. That is much more important than anything so shallow as documentary evidence."[7]

What Snodgrass does is to leave the facts of history to speak for themselves, to provide a voice (or voices) which explains the Nazis on one level. But Snodgrass, concerned with a truth beyond the facts, also rewrites history by writing poems and assigning them to dead Nazis so that there is no question about whether these poems happened or not. He thereby removes his Nazis from the past and places them in the here and now. For what purpose? To take them out of a past or future sustained by historical force or paranoia and fear. He puts the Nazis in the present, so we can look them in the eyes afresh, to see what we have not seen before.

Snodgrass's poems are not poems as if they were written by the Nazis; they were written by Snodgrass and the poems' overt formalism reminds us of this. However, if I am to show that *The Fuehrer Bunker* does, in fact, rewrite history, and if I am to show, as I believe, that this poet's choice is an ethical one—then we will need to investigate the type of history that Snodgrass writes. We'll not be further interested in the historical accuracy of the collection; rather, we'll see how history, in the figure of Old Lady Barkeep, is sustained by the collection. And we'll see how this history is unable to sustain life in the figure of Magda Goebbels. Only after this investigation of history might we then presume to apprise the ethics of the collection.

Each section of the book opens with Old Lady Barkeep. Her poems show us history is graffiti, what is written on bathroom walls or sung in streets. In fact, Old Lady Barkeep is introduced to us through a brief, parenthetical note telling us that "During World War II, Berliners revived a figure from Renaissance song and verse, Frau Wirtin, for satirical verse, similar to limericks and often obscene, about their leaders." Frau Wirtin is allowed to say things that others are not; she is able to talk about a leader with his pants down, and she shows us the price tag for the Nazi good:

> In Old Lady Barkeep's shrunken Reich
> Herr Dr. Goebbels took the mike
>   And vowed in his grand style:
> "If it costs all your lives, my dears,
> Our reign will last a thousand years!
>   Or twelve—same price. Sieg: HEIL!"

Through the person of Old Lady Barkeep, a type of history emerges to make its statement, but this history is not a consciousness, or even a structuring of cause and effect that allows the last one dead to laugh best; history is what's left of what has been sung in the barroom, the fragments of song, the memory of an obscene joke that was never funny to begin with. She may quote Goebbels, but Goebbels isn't any different than anyone else from her perspective: he's dead. "Good," we might say, "The bastard is dead. He paid the price. I'm glad that's over." But Snodgrass will complicate this response for us. From the perspective of Old Lady Barkeep, it's not over; the history of the Nazis continues because when she quotes Goebbels, he still speaks to us: "if it costs all your life."

Notice "your life," not "your lives." From the perspective of Old Lady Barkeep, we must be prepared for the possibility that the Nazis might speak to a general human condition, which Snodgrass presents as the last word in the collection:

> Old Lady Barkeep squealed with laughter
> When told she'd be forsaken after
>   Her people's sorry loss,
> She said, "There's always mobs to swallow
> Lies that flatter them and follow
>   Some savior to a cross.
>
> "Don't kid yourself—I don't play modest;
> As Greed and Cowardice's goddess,
>   I thrive on just such ruin.
> While humans prowl this globe of yours
> I'll never lack for customers.
>   By the way, how you doin'?"

The second line of the final poem clearly indicates under what conditions Old Lady Barkeep was provoked to laughter. Beginning with the second and third lines, however, readers can see their expectations diverted a bit. When will Old Lady Barkeep be forsaken? She gives two answers, as the two lines are read: (1) "after," and (2) "after / Her people's sorry loss." Answer One: In the future she will be forsaken, but when is that? Answer Two: She will be forsaken in the now of "Her people's sorry loss," but when is that?

Never, Old Lady Barkeep would reply. Because there are always mobs "to swallow," and "there's always more to swallow lies / and to follow." One might expect Old Lady Barkeep to say "follow some leader or some boss," but she tells us something quite different. There are those who will always "follow / Some savior to a cross." It isn't clear if Lady Barkeep means that those who follow will join "some savior on the cross" or if they are part of a mob following the persecution of "some savior" because, from her perspective, it doesn't matter who one follows or if one follows or is followed. In the end, Lady Barkeep enjoys either one or all. She is the voice of a history of corrigenda, of repetitions, of facts that come to no conclusion. She is the invented voice who comes disembodied from nowhere and is going nowhere, but coarsely shouts that she is exuberantly, exultantly history as it really is—and how are you doing in it?

Snodgrass frames the Nazis within this view of history. The gap between what they say they are and what Lady Barkeep says they are is evident. Only one Nazi appears to have any sense of Lady Barkeep's reality, and that is Magda Goebbels. She fears, at first, that the loss of purposefulness will undermine the choices to which she has committed her life, a loss that would render those choices (and therefore her life) meaningless.

Throughout the cycle, Frau Goebbels fears that her children might be taken from her, and—despite the fact that her children would still carry the family name beyond the war—saving her children would have been treason (15 April): "Though their survival could no doubt bring shame, / The way they'd live, They'd have to turn—once there, / Living with strangers." Yet, what kind of survival would that be "with our past that could be too much to bear." These lines are ambiguous: (1) the past might be too much for the children to bear, yes; (2) but if the children are alive, the past might be too much for Frau Goebbels to bear. Snodgrass repeats these lines in the final stanza to underscore the possibility that Frau Goebbels is speaking of herself as well:

The way they'd live, they'd have to turn, once there,
    Into the path of the Americans
With our past. *That* could be too much to bear,
    Now Joseph's sister's offered us the chance.

Snodgrass has Frau Goebbels ask a very troubling question: How can a mother make the decision not to save her children? We find the answer in the repetition of the first and third lines of the first stanza that are then repeated as the second and fourth lines of the last stanza. The first Frau Goebbels poem ends where it began, with the observation, "Now Joseph's sister has offered us the chance." She has the chance to save her children or to show the Fuehrer how nothing might remain without him. The apparent circularity of the poem shows how a call to life might be transformed into a call to death. How can Frau Goebbels save her children who will be "in the path of the Americans"? She can save them by not saving them. Logicians would no doubt identify Frau Goebbels's logic as fallacious: not all saving saves. But, as Frau Goebbels reminds us, "You ought to save the few souls dear to you, / Yet our Fuehrer would brand that as flat treason / To all we've thought, To be upright and true." Taken to its extreme, this argument leads us to assert that "not every part of life is truly life; death is also a part of life, so live with it." A question remains about how one chooses to live with death because not all deaths are created equal; some, in fact, may be "too much to bear."

In another poem (16 April), we see Frau Goebbels considering the possibility of choosing her own death. Don't leave anything behind and you will discover that the only thing left of your life is yourself. "You can destroy," Frau Goebbels observes. You can destroy the evidence (line 1); you can destroy each telltale clue (1, 6), all power to choose (1, 11), men's confidence (1, 16), the clemency (1, 21), each weakling qualm (1, 26). By line 27, destruction does not need any direct object: "You can destroy, shut down this whole / Dull little drama." By line 32, everything becomes subject to destruction: "You can destroy everything worth / Stealing from you." And, by line 37, we find that "You can destroy" can be attached to anything. "You can destroy" is also the final line of the poem,

Frau Goebbels is seeking after a fundamental joy, here, a joy that is unadulterated by some object. Each stanza of the poem demonstrates that if one destroys something that one has enjoyed—whether it be one's political craft, one's virtues, one's beauty, one's decency, one's fear, one's family—there is a purer form of enjoyment still. Even in a world devoid of everything, there is still enjoyment:

> You can destroy everything worth
> Stealing from you. Stripped and downcast,
> You can leave scarcely this scorched earth
> For them, your betters, to enjoy.
> These children? They're too good to last.
> You can destroy.

There is the pure enjoyment of death, understood here as something that one can do now, while you're alive enough to enjoy it, "You can destroy." But what kind of enjoyment is that?

Frau Goebbels's next poem (22 April) examines the problematic of this curious form of enjoyment. It is a form of enjoyment that is not possible without "the Fuehrer." We can see how the figure of Hitler serves as a guarantee that one might take enjoyment in one's own death: when there is nothing left, then there is nothing left but "our leader."

> And then I heard Him speak: our Leader, who
> Might have been talking to no one but me.
> I've got just one desire left: to be true
> Till death to Him. And what I know I'll do.

Earlier, Frau Goebbels had told us that she wanted her children "to be true." But now we see how she made that "truth" possible; she and her children might be true to Hitler:

> The children? They'll just have to come with me.
> All of us find it hard just to be true
> Till death to all this false world brings you to.

Frau Goebbels's logic will take us a little bit farther—if there is nothing but our leader, then what happens when one considers the possibility that "our leader" might not be? There is the possi-

bility of error on her part, of false judgment, and the possibility
that her children might enjoy themselves in a way that is not true:

> When they've once known our Leader? Yet if He,
> If we go, just how many could stay true?
> You try to spare them the worst misery
>
> Of wanting this, that. From our own past, we
> Know things they might have to say or do.
> How could we let them fall to treachery,
> .   .   .   .
> But they'd still want to live. What if they'd be
> Happy—they could prove all we thought untrue.
> How could we let them fall to treachery
> And their own faults? You end their misery.

Frau Goebbels leads us to consider the relationship between
enjoyment and truth. If there is some truth to the enjoyment that
we take pleasure in at this moment, the very possibility of en-
joying in some other way, even in the future, might be abhorrent.
If we even take pleasure in our children, which are our only
futures, then the only alternative is to turn away from our present
enjoyment of them and enjoy them from the perspective of something, without which, our children cannot truly exist. We throw
away our present enjoyment in order to make real the enjoyment
that we are taking in them but not at this moment.

Frau Goebbels, at this point, becomes almost a parody of a
poetic art that would take Orpheus as its progenitor: in the absence of the object there is the possibility of another form of
sublime enjoyment. This is Frau Goebbels's perverse turn in the
cycle. Outside of the history proposed by Old Lady Barkeep,
there is another history, history as that which allows us to enjoy
at the present moment. So, Frau Goebbels is willing to sacrifice
her children to this other history in order to save them, as she
tells us earlier, from the history that will require them to do
things and to accept things that would be untrue to "our
Leader"(24 April):

> Then what's your true course? Turn away;
> Look strong; they can't help but stay true.
>   You've learned what wage loyalties pay.

> Then what's your true course? Turn away
> So that they'll need you; so they'll stay
> Too scared to dare break ties with you.
> Then what's our true course? Turn away;
> Look strong; they can't help but stay true.

In this light, only the sign remains. "Our leader" becomes something other than Hitler's physical presence; "our leader" is our sign of the leader; and in terms of this sign, in the name of this sign, we are protected from error and protected from uncertainty. Magda doesn't have to worry about whether or not she should kill her children in the name of this sign. Yet, she says, "I break down sometimes, still. How can this be / The "breast that fed them once? And yet today / I wear His badge." The question, "How can this be" is both 'How can this be' that I question my decision? and 'How can this be' the breast that fed them once?" as well as 'How can this be' that I am going to kill my children? Frau Goebbels's answer is also her question. The sign or the badge isn't much help because almost anything, even opposites or contradictions, can be identified with it.

This possibility of contradictions becomes actualized in the poem of 30 April. Here, Frau Goebbels has become the "nurse who'll comfort you" and who will "free you finally from all pains / of going on in error." Under the aegis of loyalty, she has been allowed to ensure that her children will not be taken from her, that they will not be turned. Frau Goebbels even criticizes Hitler for "turning his face aside" in the end, shutting "himself in with His whore." So, suicide itself is not the answer; death is not the answer. For Frau Goebbels, there is this horrible and perfect ethical moment:

> You'll never bite the hand that fed you,
> Won't turn away from those that bred you,
> Comforted your nights and led you
>   Into the thought of virtue.
> You won't be turned from your own bed;
> Won't turn into the thing you dread;
> No new betrayal lies ahead.
>   Now no one else can hurt you.

Even Hitler cannot assume this position. Aware that Hitler is locked up with his whore, Frau Goebbels, to remain loyal to "Our leader," feels that it is she who should be alone with him. But she is alone with herself.

That is where we find her in the final "Magda Goebbels" poem. She is playing solitaire, seeing in the cards the patterns of history run along blood lines: "We build these down long lines / Like families from the Almanach / De Gotha. Of course, mine's / Pure, centuries back. / The ace." All mention of "Our leader" has disappeared. But I would say that she is still with "Him" as she understood "Him." Without her children, without something to survive her, there is only the recombination of what has gone before. Unfortunately, the cards run out. Only the player can turn the cards over and play again; in life, one might pass up something one will need later. Frau Goebbels then cheats at solitaire, but tells an imaginary child there's no harm. The cards, the relation of one thing to another in light of some system of rules, isn't enough in the final analysis. When the future is played like a game of solitaire, when history is something to be played rather than invented, look what happens. A dying woman drinks champagne, talks to an imaginary child, and plays solitaire while waiting to die. So, Frau Goebbels cannot even simply talk to herself; she must imagine a small child to instruct. Frau Goebbels found what she could not live without; it was not "Our Leader" as she had first supposed, but now after she is beyond any supposing, an imaginary child appears. Even in her last few hours, she cannot live without inventing someone to instruct.

> Sometimes you pass up just what you need. Since there's only
> Us two, we'll bring back one dead card. There; you'll
> Not scream for the police, I trust?
> This way you learn the rules;
> Don't sit and just
> Feel lonely.
>
> Still, do the best, or the worst, you can; it's all the same:
> Everything plays out on you; you're just done.
> Drink to the losses, add your score.
> Then why not try just one
> More glass, one more
> Quick game?

Frau Goebbels's last poem in the cycle has some striking similarities to the last poem in the cycle (Old Lady Barkeep, 1 May), which we have already discussed. Frau Goebbels's last poem ends with a question, as well. But, rather than ask, "How you doin'?" addressing anyone who will listen, Frau Goebbels's "you" is directed toward an imaginary child and to herself. All that matters is that one does what one can. The only hope is the possibility of just one more, the possibility that a narrative might not end, or that the last moments of one's life might be conceived of as an endless series of "just one more" half second and just one more half-of-a-half-second, and so on.

What Snodgrass has done is bring Frau Goebbels to a brick wall. He has had her do all she can do intellectually and emotionally both to save her children and remain loyal to her principles. The problematic is a maternal and paternal one, a universal one at its root. In Frau Goebbels's case, what is her response? In her own way, she achieves the perspective of history represented by Old Lady Barkeep and dreamt of by Joseph Goebbels. However, she achieves this perspective as a matter of choice—not as if killing her children were necessary as a matter of history but as if killing her children made her, albeit unintentionally, free from history—that is, true to the Fuehrer even when it is not possible to do so in this world. In another sense, she is still trapped by history; what remains of her life is caught in the movement from one card to the next, the very possibility of playing one more game. Frau Goebbels no longer has a sense of herself as someone to be seen; she is caught, laid out before herself, in the cards. Frau Goebbels is beyond death, beyond enjoyment, because she's learned to enjoy "the nothing of this world." This is not to say that she is beyond good and evil. She is, I believe, evil—although we are not accustomed to seeing "evil" in such close company with "the good" (I must save my children).

With Frau Goebbels, then, Snodgrass has given us a path that, abstractly, is not alien to us—to save our children and remain true to our principles. We have watched a mind struggle with what is good for the children, how values might be promulgated, how forces might be brought to protect them, how honor and reason should determine a parent's decisions, how difficult it is to ensure their happiness, how circumstances often intervene in well laid plans for their future—all this, which leads to a choice. Frau Goebbels does not make choices in a vacuum any more than we do. She thinks her choice to kill her children is moral and ethical. We do not. But on what grounds has Snodgrass, in *The Fuehrer Bunker* itself, established a context in which we can see that her decision need not be ours.

It seems that Snodgrass has made the making of that context, the historical moment if you will, an act of imagination, not one based upon the laws of nature or the rules of civilization or factual history, but upon a personal response to a human experience. Old Lady Barkeep sees the context as an uncodified mass, meaningful simply because it exists; Goebbels embraces a cause and effect system that encompasses both his death and its impact; Frau Goebbels plays a meaningless game that allows her act of murder to be equally meaningless, an act consistent with her own sense of morality. Such relativity extends to us. If we have not blinked away the reality of the Nazis or the histories they have created, if we have recognized them as circumstantially possible acts of imagination, then we too, in our own circumstances, can ask: who would I rather have teaching that imagined, future, child? Magda Goebbels or me?

When, in the past, I have heard colleagues speak about radicalizing literatures, they are always speaking about a novel or short story that represents someone else's misery, and they do not think it is fair that someone else should suffer as he or she does. But how far can such a simple and obvious and egocentric a morality lead one in a discussion of the Nazis? We cannot respond to the Nazi horror simply by sending a check in the mail or teaching our students about how awful things are elsewhere. And, surely, no one would be willing to suggest that the Nazis of *The Fuehrer Bunker* should not suffer. The challenge of reading *The Fuehrer Bunker* is for us to say something else about the Nazis and, I think, by implication, to say something else about evil. By focusing on the murderers, rather than their victims, Snodgrass brings the evil home. Evil is not simply a matter of other people's history, the poor souls, but a matter of how human beings relate (to/in/as) history; either history bears the burden of our good (as it does for Old Lady Barkeep) or we enjoy bearing the burden of the good of history (as does Frau Goebbels). Either way, Snodgrass's collection tells us something new about the Nazis; the imaginative fact it reveals through Old

Lady Barkeep and Magda Goebbels is the horror of total satisfaction in the pursuit of one's "good," whatever it is. Remember, even when the Fuehrer is a disappointment, Magda Goebbels learns how to save her children; even if the Nazis hadn't lost, no matter who died or lived, Old Lady Barkeep would sing ("same price"). Working out of this insight, Snodgrass manages to create a work where the emptiness and loneliness of history—not so its banality—make evil proximate to us and something we must talk about because we cannot risk being silent, as Snodgrass reminds us in the collection's next-to-the-last poem (Dr. Joseph Goebbels, 1 May 1945):

> The rest is silence. Left like sperm
> In a stranger's gut, waiting its term,
> Each thought, each step lies; the roots spread.
> They'll believe in us when we're dead.
> When we took "Red Berlin" we found
> We always worked best underground.
> So; the vile body turns to spirit
> That speaks soundlessly. They'll hear it.

We cannot risk being either alone or an empty cipher of history. Snodgrass has done his part. He has not remained neutral, as Larry Levis feared. He has not allowed the Nazis to control history. And our response? Perhaps, the poem might bear part of history's burden, our burden. We might say, as Snodgrass does about Randall Jarrell's "Protocols": "This makes the poem terribly threatening, indeed. It does not say 'He did it,' or even 'You did it'—it merely says 'This is.' It leaves open the horrifying possibility: 'I did it. We *all* did it. We all *could* do it'."[8]

Notes

1. Larry Levis, "Waiting for the End of the World: Snodgrass and *The Fuehrer Bunker*," *The Poetry of W. D. Snodgrass: Everything Human*, ed. Stephen Haven (Ann Arbor: University of Michigan Press, 1993), 281.

2. Hannah Arendt. *Origins of Totalitarianism* (New York: Harcourt, Brace & World, 1951), 469–73.

3. Paul Gaston, "W.D. Snodgrass and *The Fuehrer Bunker*: An Interview," *Papers on Language and Literature* 13, 3 (Summer 1977): 302.

4. Ibid, 303.

5. Ibid, 301.

6. Thomas Kinneally, "Preface," *Schindler's List* (New York: Simon & Schuster, 1991) .

7. Gaston, 301–2.

8. W. D. Snodgrass, "Tact and The Poet's Force," In *Radical Pursuit* (New York: Harper & Row, 1975), 15.

"They'll Hear It": W. D. Snodgrass, Walt Whitman, and the Construction of the American Consciousness

Anne Colwell

"I CELEBRATE MYSELF, AND SING MYSELF, / AND WHAT I ASSUME YOU shall assume, / For every atom belonging to me as good belongs to you."[1] In the opening lines of "Song of Myself," Walt Whitman pronounces both the essence of romantic individualism and the spiritual center of American democracy. It was part of Whitman's genius, his genius for inclusion, that he saw those two things as deeply related. W. D. Snodgrass begins his masterpiece *The Fuehrer Bunker* with a quote from Mother Teresa that could serve as an interesting commentary on Whitman's inclusiveness: "Mother Teresa, asked when it was she started her work for abandoned children, replied, 'On the day I discovered I had a Hitler inside me'." Snodgrass understands what Whitman's universal acceptance means. And his understanding of, enlarging on, and ultimately superceding Whitman's inclusiveness by daring to give voice to the Nazis, the quintessential twentieth-century example of human evil, has meant that many who fail to understand have charged him with anti-Semitism. These readers embrace the victims of the Holocaust as fully human, like themselves, but (naturally perhaps) turn away from the perpetrators as "other," separate, inhuman. This is a convenient solace for humanity that Snodgrass refuses us and himself. His insistence on inclusion like Whitman's is profoundly disconcerting; both writers admit (that is, send in) what we would hold off.

It is a truism—writers writing about each other are frequently revealing themselves. Samuel Beckett writing about James Joyce, Elizabeth Bishop writing about George Herbert, Seamus Heaney writing about W. B. Yeats, Alice Walker writing about Zora Neale

152

Hurston, they all reveal, consciously or unconsciously, their own literary concerns, passionate obsessions, and characteristic themes. They tell us what they have found in these older writers that has enriched their own creative processes. But Whitman even more than most other writers has been a touchstone for the poets that come after him and, perhaps because of the very nature of "Song of Myself," poets reveal themselves and their own predilections as they try to understand Whitman's life and work. James Wright's wonderful essay "The Delicacy of Walt Whitman" says as much about Wright and his poetic and philosophical concern with the alienated and the outsider as it does about Whitman. Similarly, W. D. Snodgrass, in his critical writings and public readings, returns again and again to Whitman. His most complete and fascinating study to date, "Whitman's Self Song," published in *The Southern Review*, focuses on Whitman's doctrine of acceptance and the ways it functions in Whitman's poetry. Snodgrass says of Whitman:

> Defining the self only by the range of its identifications, he insisted that he *was* whatever he encountered. This sense of affirmation charged not only his *Weltanschauung* but also the structure and style of his works. True, these beliefs were at times unable to overcome feelings of isolation and despair, may even have helped cause or intensify them. Yet despite Whitman's periods of despondency his work conveys a sense of sweeping and triumphant acceptance.[2]

Snodgrass goes on to examine the life events that may have necessitated Whitman's doctrine and the brilliant ways that this philosophy, however dubious, worked itself into extraordinary poetry. He sees that what he calls Whitman's positron acceptance while it "extend[s] the poet's identity" also

> demanded considerable denials and evasions: the reinvention of his saintly mother, his family situation, his health and affectional nature. And the price would get higher: in time he would have to assert that the Civil War was not really a catastrophe, that Lincoln's assassination had been a tragic sacrifice that saved the nation, that the United States could really be a force for spiritual brotherhood in the world. In short, he would be able to maintain his self-confident and cheerful belief only by shutting out larger and larger awarenesses of the dismaying reality around him.

It is the tension of opposition that Snodgrass finds at the heart of Whitman's work that I find at the heart of Snodgrass's, particularly at the heart of his latest masterpiece *The Fuehrer Bunker.* Though *The Fuehrer Bunker* and "Song of Myself" may seem, on one level, opposites, they are really inversions of each other, linked like orbiting stars by their poetic, political and social charges. Snodgrass identifies with and learns from Whitman's acceptance and inclusion, but then enlarges it, takes it where Whitman himself could not, to a deep acceptance of the human capacity for evil that Whitman's philosophy forced him to deny or to downplay. Snodgrass is not, as some contend, accepting the Nazi atrocities and their morality, but rather accepting the potential for this level of evil as present in every human being and, by giving voices to this evil, admitting it.

In his article concerning several writers and their compositional processes, "Against Your Beliefs," Snodgrass explains that "Whitman set out in "Song of Myself" to construct a doctrine, both political and metaphysical, of inclusion so he would not have to see himself as shut out from his own society, indeed from the company of the blessed."[3] However, Snodgrass argues that, in poems like "Sea Drift" and "Out of the Cradle Endlessly Rocking" as well as in diaries and day books, Whitman reveals the depths of his own despair, a despair that his doctrine of inclusion, his ecstatic acceptance of all life, could not hold off. Like Whitman, Snodgrass has set out to "construct a doctrine, both political and metaphysical, of inclusion," but for Snodgrass, as for his readers, the realization inherent in the poems is that we are not shut out from the company of the damned. Where Whitman explores the voices of the many through a celebration of his own voice, his own self, Snodgrass explores his own psyche through the voices of the many, through dramatic monologues. Snodgrass, in an interview published in the *Paris Review,* has said that the poems of the *Bunker* "may be my real confessional poems—an analysis of one's own evil."[4] It is the courage to explore the human capacity for evil, and thereby to explore his own capacity for evil, that he demonstrates by his willingness to listen to these voices; it is this courage also that he asks of his readers. In the years since World War II, as our understanding of Nazi atrocities has grown, it has been easy to relegate Hitler and his circle to isolated categories like "monster" or "anti-Christ." But genocide was not invented by the Nazis, nor did it stop with their defeat. These comforting epithets distance us from the humanity of their evil, keep us from seeing that the difference between Hitler's actions and run-of-the-mill petty hatreds is a difference in scale and not kind. For most people, it is profoundly uncomfortable to identify with the perpetrators instead of the victims, to accept that our own humanity includes both roles as possibilities in personal and historical situations.

Like Whitman, Snodgrass forces us to rethink our commonality; like Whitman, he is about creating an identity from inclusion, especially the acceptance of the rejected, the denied, "the enemy." And, also like Whitman, the identity he creates is an American identity, an American consciousness. This might seem a strange argument considering that the speakers of all of the poems are Nazis, and that the poems have been compared justly to Dante's *Inferno* for their universality and range. Pete Smith begins his article in *Agenda* with the sentence "Dangerous places need fearless guides."⁵ However, I believe the poems speak to an American audience and to the American identity in an essential and direct way. The American traditions of inclusive democracy that Whitman draws on remain deep in both our literary and mythological imaginations, and Snodgrass's version of this inclusiveness makes his poems more discomforting and more powerful in light of that heritage. Furthermore, Americans have, for decades now, constructed a kind of privileged mythology surrounding "the good war," a mythology that posits that, at least back in those "good ol' days," the evil was outside, remained foreign, and we vanquished it. These poems leave no room for that kind of comfort; as Smith argues:

One major feature of his moral strategy is to let the Nazis be fully human, have their own voices and be condemned from their own mouths. That is, to make the Nazi leaders speak so loudly and truly that we cannot help but hear what they are about. A second feature is the mirror he gives us in which to examine ourselves—a Rorschach test, if you will, on the dark side of our own psyches.

Both Snodgrass and Whitman, then, are constructing American identity through inclusion of the other, the outsider, but while

Whitman uses himself to explore the human condition, Snod-grass uses the human condition, human voices (and what voices!), to explore himself. Whitman's "Song of Myself" cele-brates the oneness of all, the hidden links between homosexual-ity and democracy, the power of life. And yet Whitman's poem, as Snodgrass himself contends, fails, just barely, to hold off despair, death, and isolation. This failure is especially evident in sections like #38 which begins "Enough! enough! enough! / Somehow I have been stunn'd. Stand back!" or section #28 which ends with "You villain touch! what are you doing? my breath is tight in its throat, / Unclench your floodgates, you are too much for me." Snodgrass's *Fuehrer Bunker* also concerns the oneness of all. It begins in many voices but calls us to hear our own voice, to recognize the humanness we share with the denizens of the bun-ker and to admit the implications of that sharing. Its many voices fail to assure either author or reader of the particularity of Nazi evil. Snodgrass, like Whitman before him, gains enormous power from the tension between inclusiveness and individuality, be-tween the particular and the universal.

In "Song of Myself" Whitman begins with the premise that he himself is the great universal that contains everything, and yet much of the power of the poem, as in the great epic catalog of section #15, comes from its particularity, the overwhelming and vivid detail. Snodgrass points out that "Whitman juxtaposes de-tails no other poet would mention with the most 'elevated' as-pects of his society, so making his best catalogs not only 'democratic' but startling and vivid throughout":

> The pure contralto sings in the organ loft,
> The carpenter dresses his plank, the tongue of his foreplane
> whistles its wild ascending lisp,
> The married and unmarried children ride home to their
> Thanksgiving dinner,
> The pilot seizes the king-pin, he heaves down with a strong arm,
> The mate stands braced in the whale-boat, lance and harpoon are
> ready.

In contrast, *The Fuehrer Bunker* begins with the premise that we are listening to particular voices, monologues—the imagined speech of real historical people who are not us. But these monologues are different from any other dramatic monologues I know, first because of what Ben Howard called their "virtuosic display of received and invented forms,"[6] and second because of their effect, their ability to undermine the barriers between reader and speaker.

Snodgrass has for years been a master of form and his earlier books, from the Pulitzer Prize-winning *Heart's Needle* to *Each in His Season*, have all demonstrated his ability to astonish the language into its own power through rhyme and meter. But Snodgrass's symphony of form in *The Fuehrer Bunker* is not about displaying his virtuosity. His own assessment of Whitman offers a better clue to the need for form in the *Bunker*:

> I find it very surprising, however, and far-reaching in implication, that Whitman, like Hopkins, when he moved from a poem of joyous belief to one of anguished questioning, should also move from a loose and open metrical form to one more rigid and demanding. For the "Song of Myself" with its doctrine of inclusion—inclusion of all forbidden subject matter, of all levels of language and vocabulary, all modes of image and sound texture—a sort of polymorphous perverse prosody was adequate. . . . For the later, despairing poem, however, for the discovery that his torment was not quieted, that the world was even more various and chaotic than dreamed of in his philosophy, he needed a more fixed form.[7]

Snodgrass argues that Whitman could "no more adapt to his society's literary practices than to its mating rituals—its strict couplets, if you will," but he notes that even in "Song of Myself," "Readers may be surprised by how often Whitman appropriates the customary and time honored modes."

When Elizabeth Bishop wrote the first draft of her famous villanelle, "One Art," which concerns the painful process of loss in her own life, she began in free verse. The draft deteriorated into a repetition of the negatives "no" and "never again." At the bottom of the page, she began to play with the villanelle rhyme scheme. One of the things that poetic form can do is hold the impossibly chaotic and various still for one moment. And by showing us how tenuous that hold is, how weak and brief our own order looks, poetic form also points out, ironically, how powerful the forces of chaos are. This notion is crucially important to the *Bunker* because Snodgrass's pantoums, villanelles, triolets, and couplets, as well as his invented platoons and files, bring the voices of the speakers to life, comment on those voices, and also point out the tenuous nature of the boundary between their voices and our own.

For example, in Magda Goebbels's poem of 30 April she speaks to the children she is about to kill, rationalizing her actions. The *aaabcccb* rhyme scheme and the even meter mimic a fairy tale and the tone of comforting assurance that we've all heard, all used to quiet upset children:

> This is the needle that we give
> Soldiers and children when they live
> Near the front, in primitive
>   Conditions or real dangers;
> This is the spoon we use to feed
> Men trapped in trouble or in need,
> When weakness or bad luck might lead
>   Them to the hands of strangers.

The form of the poem both creates and comments on Magda Goebbels's voice and motivations; it makes momentary sense out of the unreasonable passions surrounding her murderous acts. The form and the tone it establishes, through its simple rhymes, even meter, and its "House-That-Jack Built" repetitive naming, also allows us to hear our own voices in her voice.

This tenuous boundary between voices is another quality that separates these poems from other, more traditional, dramatic monologues. The position of the reader relative to the poem's speaker seems quite different from that in, say, Browning's "My Last Duchess" or even T. S. Eliot's "The Love Song of J. Alfred Prufrock." In both of these traditional monologues the reader is allowed an ironic distance from the speaker that creates the effect of the poem. For example, in Browning's poem, the reader listens to the Duke speak and as the Duke's words betray him, the reader gradually comes to realize that the Duke is a monster. By the time the Duke pronounces "—E'en then would be some stooping; and I choose / Never to stoop" we have seen through his pomposity to the fullblown evil of his murderousness. In the final lines, the contradiction "Nay, we'll go / together down, sir" puts the reader firmly in the position of the emissary from the Count of Tyrol, trying to escape the Duke, or warn the Count of the Duke's monstrosity. The implied threat of the words "go together down" cannot wash over into self-realization for the reader because the reader, like the emissary, has been given a position of moral superiority.

Eliot begins "The Love Song of J. Alfred Prufrock" with a quote from Dante that might call into question the reader's ironic distance: "If I thought that I was speaking / to someone who would go back to the world, / this flame would shake no more." However, we know that Dante, like Eliot's reader, will go back, is still beyond hell, distanced enough to have some perspective. By the final lines of the monologue we stand in a morally superior position, able to see what Prufrock cannot, that he has missed his opportunity at life. The difference between our position as reader in these monologues and in *The Fuehrer Bunker* is that, when Snodgrass is our Virgil, we are not passing through for a lesson, but being shown the hell that we inhabit.

Like Whitman, Snodgrass seeks to annihilate and recreate the American identity through inclusion. As readers of these dramatic monologues, we have the comforting blanket of ironic distance snatched away from us and are confronted, not with what *they* are, but with who *we* are, or who we may become. In order to close that ironic distance, Snodgrass must work very hard, particularly because, as Americans, we've internalized the lesson that these are the voices of monsters, the quintessential evil. To overcome this easy reaction, Snodgrass uses several techniques that challenge his readers' preconceptions: he employs polyphony within poems; he demonstrates (in the manner of classical tragedy) how admirable human qualities, skewed, can prove more destructive than vices; and, finally, he directly accuses the reader of complicity.

Snodgrass's use of voices within voices, polyphony, undermines the reader's ability to label the voice as other and dismiss it. We are uncomfortably aware that this is not one monstrous voice but a collection of voices that we recognize and even accept as our own. In this way polyphony also points out for the reader the connection between these voices and voices that the culture reveres. Eva Braun's poem of 22 April provides a good example of this strategy. The epigraph to the poem explains that "(His mistress's small revenges for Hitler's neglect included singing

American songs, her favorite being 'Tea for Two.' Having chosen
to die with him in the bunker, she seemed serene during the last
days)." The stanzas of the monologue in which Eva Braun speaks
are broken up by quotations from the popular American song.
The poem becomes a commentary, not just on the power struggle
and sickness of the relationship between Braun and Hitler, but
on the potential for this same sickness in all romantic relation-
ships. For example, the seemingly innocent lines from the song
"Nobody near us / To see us or hear us" introduce and illuminate
a stanza in which Braun relishes her triumph over her rivals:

> I have it all. They are all gone, the others—
> The Valkyrie; and the old rich bitch Bechstein;
> Geli above all. No, the screaming mobs above all.
> They are all gone now. He has left them all.
> No one but me and the love-struck secretaries—
> Traudl, Daran—who gave up years ago.

In the next lines of the song, we hear an echo in another chord
but of the same statement of aloneness: "No friends or relations /
On weekend vacations." The innocence of the popular song does
not stand apart as easy ironic comment; instead Snodgrass's technique calls into question the cultural structure of romantic rela-
tionships through this particular relationship. When I taught this
poem to a group of university sophomores the tensions between
the audience's expectations and the poem's commentary became
very clear to me. The question most repeated, like an incantation
against the evil, was "But does she really love him?" Many of the
students sought to define the relationship as other than romantic,
wanted a solution that said "These kinds of power games are
never a part of love." But the poem insistently combines the
crooner's voice, the seemingly innocent romantic, with the voice
of sexual conqueror in a way that implicates the romantic. We
are asked to look closely at our culture's and our own ideas of
love and to see if the human potential for destruction is not
embedded (pun intended) in them. This juxtapositioning shows
us that the darkness is not other, but a constant human option.

This strategy becomes even more evident and more frightening
at the end of the poem, when the reader realizes that Braun's
serenity comes from a sense of having attained ultimate triumph,
not only over her rivals for Hitler's love, but over Hitler himself,

and thereby over all whom Hitler has killed. She has forced him
to acknowledge her in public, and her final stanza is introduced
by the song lyrics "For me to take / For all the boys to see." The
last lines of the poem foreshadow Hitler's own insistence at the
moment of his suicide that he is still "winning":

> Once more I have won, won out over Him
> Who spoke one word and whole populations vanished.
> Until today, in public, we were good friends.
> He is mine. No doubt
> I did only what He wanted; no doubt
> I should resent that. In the face
> Of such fulfillment? In the face
> Of so much joy?

> Picture you
> Upon my knee;
> Tea for two
> And two for tea . . .

The connections between the ideas in the song and the ideas
in Braun's monologue undermine the reader's ability to dismiss
Braun and Hitler's relationship as an isolated and sick anomaly,
and instead point out that the roots of their power struggle are
neither particular to them nor particular to Germans. The final
quotation of the song lyric works like an overlay to demonstrate
the power play of romance; who is upon whose knee?

Similarly, Hitler's final monologue of 30 April employs at least
five distinct voices rendered by typeface and indentation: Hitler's
public speaking voice, a voice that tallies his score in numbers
of dead, quotations from his favorite Disney films, quotations
from the grail quest in *Lohengrin*, and a voice of his own internal
ranting. The polyphony of Hitler's final poem not only suggests
the instability of his identity, but also shows the tenuous boundaries between his voice and other voices that the culture reveres,
or at least perceives as innocent:

> **Deceived! Deceived! Shamelessly Deceived!**
> **Betrayal! Betrayal! Exceeding all revenge!**

> Pole: three million.

> "Casualties never can be high enough.

They are the seeds of future heroism."

> And seven at one blow, one blow,
> And seven at one blow.

The introduction of the Disney voice, like the inclusion of "Tea for Two" in Eva Braun's poem, has particular moment for the American reader because it implicates what Americans hold up as an innocent and childlike part of their own culture. Americans have always valued innocence as one of the essential qualities that separates our culture from the culture of European decadence, and American literature and popular media alike, from Henry James to Huck Finn to *Free Willy*, hold up childlike innocence and purity of belief as true American values. Snodgrass's mixing of Disney songs and Hitler's voices in this poem is not just a reflection of a peculiar historical fact, Hitler did have favorite Disney movies, but an indication of American complicity in creating the Nazi regime. Like Whitman in "Song of Myself," Snodgrass must overcome or undermine the barriers that we have erected between self and other. Snodgrass's polyphony works much like Whitman's sensuous catalogs to open us to the other before we have had time to consciously defend against it. Commenting on Whitman's strategy in the catalogs of "Song of Myself" Snodgrass quotes Whitman's lines:

> The prostitute draggles her shawl, her bonnet bobs on her tipsy
> and pimpled neck,
> The crowd laugh at her blackguard oaths, the men jeer and wink at
> each other,
> (Miserable! I do not laugh at your oaths nor jeer you;)
> The President holds a cabinet council, he is surrounded by the
> great secretaries,
> On the piazza walk five friendly matrons with twined arms;
> the crew of the fish-smack pack repeated layers of halibut in the
> hold,

and explains that "Present day readers may well miss the boldness, the offense against decorum in both subject matter and juxtaposition." Snodgrass, in *The Fuehrer Bunker*, has made just such an offense against modern day sensibility. Maybe this explains the strange tendency for usually enlightened readers to haul out the damning charge of anti-Semitism. He also employs juxtaposition, but juxtaposition of voices, to shock present day readers out of their complacency. In discussing Whitman's strategy, he goes on to note that "Just as we cannot fully hear Beethoven's music—or even Debussy's—unless we re-create in our minds the environment of expected harmony into which that music had to assert itself, so we cannot realize how Whitman sounded to readers (or even to himself) without partially replicating the literary atmosphere of the mid-nineteenth century." We are in the atmosphere, the literary moment, to which Snodgrass speaks, and that closeness can mean its own kind of blindness, or at least myopia.

Snodgrass has set out to undermine and change this short-sightedness. He seeks to shatter our position of moral superiority by creating voices that hold out some of our own values, but then show how those values can easily be twisted into evil. Like a classical tragedian, Snodgrass demonstrates that even what we accept as good can be turned. Helga Goebbels's poem of 29 April reflects her understanding of many of the values that all parents set out to inculcate in their children, obedience, bravery, loyalty. But here, as she reflects on the killing of Blondi's puppies (Blondi was Hitler's dog), the child's two voices, that of the ardent Nazi she becomes to make up for being a girl and that of the frightened girl, demonstrate how these values, just slightly askew, become as monstrous as any shortcoming:

> They'd not get fed or cared for here;
> > *I stayed to hear our Uncle Fuehrer*
> Strangers would just chase them away.
> > *When the rest skipped out to play.*
> Our Fuehrer, history's greatest man,
> > *Father's sister might take them in*
> Shows how true faith and steadfastness
> > *Only they'd make her house a mess.*
>
> Hardens us for harsh tasks. He teaches
> > *Blondi snarled: no one could touch*
> Those hurt past all help need a hand
> > *Her young. She didn't understand.*
> To end their pain. Nobody would
> > *I tried: I wanted to be good.*
> Want life where there's no faith, no love.

> *Father, forgive me. Let me live.*

The child's brave reasoning in the pica type voice perfectly mirrors the reasoning that her mother will use to bring herself to kill the child. The italic voice ironically demonstrates that Blondi proves a better and more protective mother to her pups than Helga's own mother does to her children and reflects the child's understanding of the horrible dilemma of love and loyalty in which she finds herself. The essence of human tragedy, from the Greeks to the Shoah to the present, comes not just from our shortcomings or our evil, but from our best qualities exercised without moderation or in the wrong situations. The real terror of many of these poems derives from the values that the speakers espouse rather than from any lack of value.

Magda Goebbels's poems return repeatedly to the virtue of loyalty, insisting that she above all others understands loyalty to one's leader and possesses the ability to be steadfast when all around him fail. From the capitalization of the pronouns He and Him when they refer to Hitler, the reader comes to understand that her leader has become her God. The opening lines of her poem from 27 April illustrate her pride in her loyalty, and the complex constructions of the self that underpin this pride:

> I wear His badge, here, on my breast today;
> > All those lost years, He must have wanted me.
> I've borne old sacrifices; I obey.
> > I stand restored: His heir, His deputy.

The end of the poem reveals that this virtuous loyalty is far worse than any vice as it will lead Magda to kill her own children:

> Though I'm their keeper, too. I can't help see
> > Their eyes wavering toward me while they play.
> I break down sometimes, still. How can this be
> > The breast that fed them once? And yet today
> > > I wear His badge.

In the second line, Magda Goebbels projects the "wavering" onto the children, and then admits briefly that she herself breaks down. However, by reasserting her status as deputy, she regains her self-created symbolic role as the ever-faithful, the chosen of

God. This poem has resonances with some of the most important vehicles for the culture's values, including folktales of the steadfast friend, American Westerns, and the entire Christian structure of martyrdom. Therefore, the terror of the poem comes, not from its lack of values, but from the values that it demonstrates so clearly, and from how close those values are to our own, or at least to our culture's.

It should not be surprising to us then, when, at the end of the cycle, both Joseph Goebbels's poem of 1 May and Old Lady Barkeep, the chorus figure, directly accuse us of participating in this evil. If, up to this point in the cycle, the reader has allowed his or her complicity to remain a nagging but unconscious notion, the last stanza of Goebbels's poem brings it to light:

> The rest is silence. Left like sperm
> In a stranger's gut, waiting its term,
> Each thought, each step lies; the roots spread.
> They'll believe in us when we're dead.
> When we took "Red Berlin" we found
> We always worked best underground.
> So; the vile body turns to spirit
> That speaks soundlessly. They'll hear it.

Goebbel's declaration that the Nazi spirit will "Pass on, and infect history" recalls, in negative, Whitman's declaration at the end of "Song of Myself":

> I bequeath myself to the dirt to grow from the grass I love,
> If you want me again look for me under your boot-soles.
>
> You will hardly know who I am or what I mean,
> But I shall be good health to you nevertheless,
> And filter and fibre your blood.
>
> Failing to fetch me at first keep encouraged,
> Missing me one place search another,
> I stop somewhere waiting for you.

Both poems suggest that inclusion not only overleaps the obstacle of death but is actually augmented by death. Both suggest that the spirit "speaks soundlessly" beyond the confines of the now defunct body. Both directly implicate the reader in the construction of the doctrine of inclusion. The last sentences of each are mirror images of each other, Whitman's suggesting the inevitable joy of connection, Snodgrass's the inevitable poisoning of connection. In some ways, Goebbels's declaration of connection and inclusion is odd, for the drama of these characters has been one of peculiar and terrible isolation, never speaking to, only commenting on each other. In fact, their deeply isolated bunker with its further isolated chambers becomes emblem and metaphor for the psyches and souls, if you will, of these characters. But Goebbels's connection is the same as Whitman's in many ways. As Snodgrass points out,

> The inclusive ego may, of course, have less admirable aspects. . . . the question remains whether, so incorporated, difference has been preserved or merely homogenized and obliterated. We know that Whitman's siblings found his authority "excessive"; we wonder if they might not have preferred to be buried separately, under their own names. . . . Omnisexuality like democracy, promises equality, but that equality may be hollow, each of its objects rendered insignificant. We recall that most promises of universal love and comradeship have led to spiritual cannibalism.

David Reynolds, one biographer of Whitman, quotes Pablo Neruda, who calls Whitman "the first totalitarian poet" and says "Indeed, there is a despotic force in Whitman's theory and practice of poetry: 'What I assume you shall assume'."[8]

Where Whitman searches out the other for inclusion in the varied universe of the self, Goebbels' searches out the other in order to subsume it. How different is this? But, if there is a hidden threat in Whitman's "I stop somewhere waiting for you," there is also a hidden redemption in "They'll hear it." For if we remain capable of hearing it, of hearing our own voices in these voices, we still remain capable of fighting it. Perhaps we do not, like Mother Teresa, dedicate our lives to working for the poor, but we may, in our own ways, identify and refuse to follow the Hitler inside us.

Old Lady Barkeep, a figure from Renaissance song and verse that Berliners resurrected for often obscene, satirical poems, gets the last word in *The Fuehrer Bunker*. Her limericklike verse explicitly points a finger at the reader:

> Old Lady Barkeep squealed with laughter
> When told she'd be forsaken after
>   Her people's sorry loss.
> She said, "There's always mobs to swallow
> Lies that flatter them and follow
>   Some savior to a cross.

> "Don't kid yourself—I don't play modest;
> As Greed and Cowardice's goddess,
>   I thrive on just such ruin.
> While humans prowl this globe of yours
> I'll never lack for customers.
>   By the way, how *you* doin'?

Her final question is both the most damning and the most potentially saving question in the cycle. For Old Lady Barkeep directly accuses all humans of complicity in the horror, but simultaneously she gives us an opportunity to own up to and thereby, at least for a few moments, recognize and perhaps thwart some of the evil we ourselves are capable of. In this way, Snodgrass goes beyond Whitman's inclusiveness by accepting all human possibility as his own. Not just the possibility of human despair, the bedraggled prostitute, the suicide, who sin against the social mores, but also the possibility of our human hatred and violence that destroys even our own kind on a level both imaginable and real.

It seems to me beautifully ironic and perfectly fitting that, while "Song of Myself," one of the most redemptive and positive poetic pronouncements on human nature, carries its own threat of despair, *The Fuehrer Bunker*, one of the most damning poetic indictments of human nature, carries within it its own potential for salvation. Both Snodgrass and Whitman communicate a human reality too large for either damnation or salvation alone, for either despair or optimism. They push the limits of the American consciousness and American identity to include all human possibilities. That is why we can say, as D. H. Lawrence said of Whitman, that Americans must work to be "worthy of their"

Snodgrass, and why neither *The Fuehrer Bunker* nor "Song of Myself" are finally American only.

Snodgrass's final comment on Whitman in "Whitman's Selfsong" could apply equally to his own work:

> Is any of us so simple, so monolithic, that he or she can tell the world plainly and directly, "This is who I am"? Is any of us so deadly dull, so brain-damaged, as to have no deeps or dungeons hidden out of sight if not out of mind? Yet how many of us can claim that our reticences, our disguises, our lies and myths, have revealed so much, have produced such rich and rewarding results?

In seeking to understand the human ability to destroy our own kind Snodgrass has revealed not just human evil but its opposite, the great good in our own capacity for self-awareness, self-critical reflection, and choice.

Notes

1. Walt Whitman, *Leaves of Grass*, eds. Harold W. Blodgett and Sculley Bradley (New York: W. W. Norton and Company, 1965).

2. W. D. Snodgrass, "Whitman's Selfsong," *The Southern Review* 32, 3 (Summer 1996): 572.

3. W. D. Snodgrass, "Against Your Beliefs." *The Southern Review* 26, 3 (Summer 1990): 492.

4. W. D. Snodgrass, "Interview," *Paris Review*, Spring 1994: 187.

5. Pete Smith, "The Rorschach Bunker," *Agenda* (Spring 1996): 112.

6. Ben Howard, "a review of *Each in His Season*," *Poetry* (1989): 97.

7. "Against your Beliefs," 493.

8. David S. Reynolds, *Walt Whitman's America: A Cultural Biography* (New York: Alfred A. Knopf, 1995), 49.

Contributors

BERNARD BENSTOCK was past president of the international James Joyce Foundation and editor of the *James Joyce Literary Supplement*. He was Professor of English at the University of Miami and the author of a dozen books on Joyce. His *Joyce Again's Wake* was among the first critical studies of *Finnegans Wake*. The author of numerous other books, articles, and reviews, Professor Benstock ranged widely in his studies of modern and contemporary literature. His essay on W. D. Snodgrass was one of his final pieces.

ZACK BOWEN is Professor of English at the University of Miami. He edits the *James Joyce Literary Supplement*, and is the general editor of the Joyce Series as well as the Critical Essays in British Literature Series. His books include *Padraic Colum, Mary Lavin, Musical Allusions in the Works of James Joyce, A Reader's Guide to John Barth*, and *Bloom's Old Sweet Song*. He is also the author of more than a hundred essays, notes, and reviews on modern British and American literature.

FRED CHAPPELL teaches at the University of North Carolina-Greensboro. He has received the Bollingen Prize in Poetry, the Award in Literature from the National Institute of Arts and Letters, the Best Foreign Novel Prize from the French Academy, and numerous other awards. His *Spring Garden: New and Selected Poems* appeared in 1995, and in 1996 he published a new novel, *Farewell, I'm Bound to Leave You*. He is at work on a translation of the *Alcestis* of Euripides.

ANNE COLWELL's book, *Inscrutable Houses: Metaphors of the Body in the Poems of Elizabeth Bishop*, was published in 1997. She works as an Assistant Professor of English for the University of Delaware in the Georgetown Parallel Program. Her poems have appeared in several journals including *Eclectic Literary Forum, Southern Poetry Review, Dominion Review,* and *Midwest Quarterly Review.*

PETER MAKUCK is Distinguished Professor of Arts and Sciences at East Carolina University where he has taught and edited *Tar River Poetry* since 1976. In 1990–91 he was the Visiting Writer at Brigham Young University. His essays, stories, and poems have appeared in *Poetry, The Southern Review, The Hudson Review, The Sewanee* Review, and *The Virginia Quarterly Review.* He is the co-editor of *An Open World: Essays on Leslie Norris.* His fifth volume of poetry, *Against Distance,* was published by BOA Editions Ltd. in 1997.

DAVID METZGER is an Assistant Professor of English at Old Dominion University. He is the editor of the Lacan journal *Bien Dire,* has edited a forthcoming issue of *Pre/Text,* and is the co-editor of a forthcoming collection of essays entitled "Reading and Writing in the New Middle Ages." He has published essays on medieval and Renaissance rhetorical theory, ancient nonclassical rhetorics, and myth. He is currently cowriting a textbook on the Bible as literature, as well as finishing a book on ancient Egyptian rhetoric.

DEVON MILLER-DUGGAN studied at Mount Holyoke College, received an M.A. from the Writing Seminars at Johns Hopkins University, and completed her Ph.D at the University of Delaware. Her dissertation is titled "After Auschwitz: Response and Responsibility in American Holocaust Poetry." Her poetry has appeared in *Indiana Review, Shenandoah, Cut Bank, Gargoyle,* and elsewhere. She lives in Newark, Delaware.

JAMES OLNEY is co-editor of *The Southern Review* and author of *Metaphors of Self, The Rhizome and the Flower, Tell Me Africa,* and *The Language(s) of Poetry.* He has recently completed a book titled *Memory and Narrative,* which is a study of the two title subjects in life-writing from St. Augustine to Samuel Beckett.

PHILIP RAISOR has taught at Old Dominion University since 1969. His essays on Arnold, Browning, Joyce, Faulkner, and contemporary poetry have appeared in *Studies in English Literature, Tennessee Studies in Literature, South Dakota Review, Contemporary Literature,* and elsewhere. His poetry and interviews have appeared in, among others, *The Southern Review, Poetry Northwest, Tar River Poetry, The Midwest Quarterly.* He is a former managing editor of the *New Virginia Review.*

BRENDA TREMBLAY is a radio producer for WXXI, a public broadcasting station in Rochester, New York. Her radio features air regularly on National Public Radio, and she has produced several documentaries about poetry and music. She is a 1990 graduate of Houghton College in Houghton, New York. She lives with her husband Don in a small town near Lake Ontario.

Index